Autumn Quail

NAGUIB MAHFOUZ

Autumn Quail

Translated by
Roger Allen
Revised by
John Rodenbeck

The American University in Cairo Press

To Mary

INTRODUCTION

The stature which Naguib Mahfouz has earned as the Arab
world's most illustrious novelist is well captured by 'Abd al-
Rahman Yaghi when he entitles the fourth chapter of his
book *Al-Juhud al-Riwa'iyya* (*Endeavors in the Novel*, 1972) "The
Novel's Establishment Stage, in other words the Naguib
Mahfouz Stage." Several studies of his works in English have
by now been added to the myriad books, articles, and inter-
views on him which have appeared throughout the Arab world
itself. While he is not yet as well known to Western readers
as some other famous non-Western writers, several of his
works are available in English and a number of others are to
appear shortly.*

The word for "establishment" in Yaghi's title quoted above
is *ta'sil*, which literally implies giving something roots. That
describes very well the role which Mahfouz has played in the
development of the modern Arabic novel. Throughout a long
career he has indeed laid the groundwork for the emergence
of this most taxing and variegated genre and then proceeded
to experiment with a number of forms and techniques. Some
scholars have chosen to divide his works into "phases," each
one with its specific characteristics; others have preferred to
illustrate the continuum of themes which occupy the author's
mind, pointing out at the same time that features of these
"phases" will often have been presaged in earlier writings. In
spite of the differences between these viewpoints, both ac-

*A listing of many of these works and translations into English can be found in my
book *The Arabic Novel: An Historical and Critical Introduction* (Syracuse: Syracuse University Press, 1982).

knowledge that Mahfouz has been constantly striving to find new ways to express his vision of Egypt's present and therefore its past and future. This remains as true of his most recent writings, where, in addition to his continuing experiments with multi-sectional works and a variety of narrative voices, we find echoes of earlier Arabic literature, such as *The Thousand and One Nights* and the travels of Ibn Battuta.

During the 1960s, Mahfouz wrote a great deal: novels, short stories, and plays. Much of the inspiration for this outburst of creativity was certainly prompted by the wide success of his monumental three-part novel, *Al-Thulathiyya* (*The Trilogy*, 1956–57). And yet it is also abundantly clear from his writings in all the genres listed above that an equally cogent force impelling him to write was a deep disquiet with the course of the Egyptian revolution, a feeling which was to be vented at its fullest in *Miramar* (1967) and in works published after the June war of 1967. With that in mind it is of some interest to note that Mahfouz chose in the second of the novels of this decade, *Al-Summan wal-Kharif* (*Autumn Quail*, 1962) to indulge in a historical retrospect by placing the action of the novel during the Revolution of 1952 itself and the years immediately following. Thus, while this work may be something of an anomaly within the sequence of Mahfouz's works conceived and written during the 1960s, it surely possesses considerable significance as one of the very few works to treat the events of the Revolution itself within a fictional context.

The novel opens with a description of the famous Cairo fire which followed the massacre of Egyptian policemen at the Suez Canal by British soldiers in January 1952. It goes on to trace (often through the medium of radio broadcasts) the main events of the early stages of the Revolution—the purge of corrupt officials and the abolition of political parties, for example. It comes to an end sometime after the nationalization of the Suez Canal Company and the Tripartite (British, French, and Israeli) invasion of 1956. There is also a very concrete link to place in this work: to various districts of Cairo, each with its own memories and connotations; and to Alexandria, with its pounding winter seas, its foreign quarters, and its still much desired distance from the clamor of the capital city. Thus, of all the novels which Mahfouz published in the 1960s, *Autumn Quail* has the strongest connection with the realities of both time and place.

Against the backdrop of these places and events, the central character whose fall is portrayed in this novel is Isa ad-Dabbagh, a senior civil servant in the Egyptian government during the final days of the monarchy. He has just become engaged to Salwa, the beautiful and feckless daughter of Ali Bey Sulaiman, a justice and senior Palace official. Isa and his mother live in an opulent villa in Dokki, then as now a typical outward symbol of the *nouveau arrivé*. The graphic description of the Cairo fire—with its sinister symbols of smoke and fire—warns of dire things to come. Sure enough, after the revolution comes the Purge Committee. Isa's past willingness to accept bribes catches up with him, and he is pensioned off. As a result of this loss of position and prestige his engagement to Salwa is abruptly terminated.

Isa is of course a symbol of all that the immediate past stands for. In his defense before the Purge Committee he excuses himself by pointing out that everyone behaved exactly as he did, and asks why it is that he is being singled out. However, in spite of Isa's rapid and heavy fall, the past which he symbolizes throughout the novel does manage to display positive characteristics as well. For, unlike his friend Ibrahim Khairat, who almost immediately sets about penning hypocritical articles in praise of the revolution, Isa remains stubbornly loyal to the old regime and adamantly refuses to consider accepting the offer of a job from his cousin Hasan, who has become an important figure because of the revolution. This positive aspect of Isa's character, his sense of loyalty and concern for his country, is perhaps best seen through his relationship with Qadriyya, the woman whom he eventually marries. At the outset Isa is aware that the marriage may not work and leaves himself an escape route by overlooking her previous marriages. But as the couple live together through the Suez Crisis of 1956, Isa is amazed by her total lack of concern with politics and the fate of Egypt. Qadriyya, the barren, overfed nonentity, brings out the positive side of Isa's attitude.

On the intellectual level Isa seems to become reconciled to the idea of accepting the revolution and the changes which it is bringing about. But on every occasion his basic emotional instincts hold him back, at least until the very end of the novel. He suffers an internal conflict between mind and emotion, and it is in the latter area that the women of the novel play such an important role. If the marriage to Qadriyya, with its literal and figurative barrenness, is doomed from the start, then the relationship with Riri, the Alexandrian prostitute, represents Isa's real fight with emotion, his total failure to meet his moral responsibilities, and his eventual realization through a very bitter lesson of what those responsibilities are. This relationship is as creative—literally—as that with Qadriyya is not. Isa's failure to regain his real family (as he comes to call it) symbolizes the failure of his emotions to react responsibly to the circumstances in which his own past has left him. As he realizes this bitter fact and its consequences for the future, his life with Qadriyya emerges as the sham which it really is and always has been; in his own words, he has no home with her.

The final pages bring Isa together with a young man whom he had imprisoned during his period as a powerful civil servant. By now, his emotions have been jolted into some kind of reality by the sight of his own daughter and by Riri's bitter words to him. Past and present encounter each other in the dark under the statue of Saad Zaghlul, the poignant symbol of the past mentioned several times in this book and with equal effect in *Miramar*. Isa is disturbed and troubled by the young man's friendly attitude and by his enthusiasm for the revolution. When the latter gives up hope of converting Isa and heads toward the city, Isa follows him. Since it is past midnight, this may perhaps be considered a move away from Saad Zaghlul's statue, out of the darkness toward some new dawn.

From an artistic point of view, this ending—with Isa running after the young man into an uncertain future—has been regarded as contrived. We have already noted that Isa had given several signs of a dispassionate *intellectual* acceptance of the revolution. The question to be posed in the current context thus concerns his stubborn adherence to his own past and his emotional attitudes. What is the role of his final encounters with Riri and his own daughter, Ni'mat, in this process? Has it shaken him into a sense of emotional and moral responsibility sufficient to justify his decision to run after the young man? Is the Indian palm reader's comment about "recovery from a serious illness" a forewarning of his eventual decision to follow the young man? I must leave it to the readers of *Autumn Quail* to make their own judgments on the *artistic* efficacy of the ending vis-à-vis these questions; I would merely comment that I find it less unconvincing than many of its critics do.

The long period of time (over four years) covered by this novel, the close linkage with the political events of the day, and the optimistic ending have all been criticized on artistic, if not political, grounds. It has been suggested that *Autumn Quail* represents a response on Mahfouz's part to critical reactions (including presumably those of "the official cultural sector" of which he himself was a part) to the subtly negative commentary on the Revolution to be found in *Al-Liss wal-Kilab* (*The Thief and the Dogs*, 1961), the first novel in the series of works published in the 1960s. In the latter work, a man who has been "framed" is released from prison and vows vengeance on his wife and her lover, who have tricked him. In trying to kill them, he mistakenly kills two other people and is then hunted (or hounded) down by the police as a homicidal maniac, meeting his death in a cemetery as the police dogs chase after him. *Autumn Quail* certainly represents —at least in the implications of its ending—a more "upbeat" view of Egyptian society than that. I would not wish to imply that Mahfouz felt himself to be under the same constraints as Dimitri Shostakovich, who prefaced his Fifth Symphony with the phrase "an artist's response to just criticism" in the wake of his ostracism from Russian cultural life (in turn a reaction to his Fourth Symphony). However, one may legitimately wonder whether the general intellectual atmosphere in Egypt during the early 1960s—a period about which many details concerning assaults on civil liberties have only recently come to light—did not suggest to Mahfouz that a retrospect with positive contemporary implications might be at least apropos.

Whatever the artistic and societal motivations may have been in writing *Autumn Quail*, Mahfouz decided to trace within a novelistic framework the relationship of past and present within the Egyptian Revolution and the possibilities of co-operation, or perhaps coexistence, in the future. It has to be admitted that the novel's narrative suffers from the extended time period. Bearing in mind Isa's frequent travel back and forth between Cairo and Alexandria, the links of time and place seem to be extended beyond endurance in a comparatively short novel (compared, for example, with *The Trilogy*, a huge societal canvas in which these two aspects can be more expansively and successfully managed).

All this said, *Autumn Quail* will provide the Western reader with insights and reflections on the Egyptian Revolution and its progress, put into the mouths of Egyptian characters from different backgrounds and with varying social and political attitudes. Indeed, several themes of this work—alienation, political downfall, moral responsibility, to name a few—transcend the boundaries of independent national literary traditions and are to be found in much of contemporary world fiction. As for the characters themselves (quite apart from the intrinsic interest of their comments about politics, religion, and the world situation), the symbolic mesh within which Mahfouz illustrates their relationships gives this work a peculiar fascination.

ROGER ALLEN

Autumn Quail

ONE

When the train drew to a halt, he could see no one waiting for him. Where was his secretary? Where were the office staff and the messengers? He looked among the people standing outside on the platform but failed to find anyone he recognized. What had happened? At the Canal the blow had been vicious, but was Cairo reeling as well?

He left his place in the front of the carriage and walked toward the exit, briefcase in hand, feeling irritated and tense, then worried, until, driven by some natural impulse, he began to examine people's faces closely. They seemed to mirror a terrifying anxiety. He himself felt apprehensive. What was the cause? The massacre at the Canal the day before or some new miseries on the way? Should he ask people what was going on? No one had been waiting for him; nobody from his office had taken the trouble to come and meet him. Incredible behavior! These were strange days indeed.

His mind still held the bloody scenes at the Canal, the slaughtered policemen, their defenseless heroism. He still heard the earsplitting shouts of the young commando: "Where are you people? Where's the government? Weren't you the ones who proclaimed the holy war?"

"Yes!" he'd replied in anguish. "That's why I'm standing here in the middle of nowhere."

The young man had turned on him. "What we need is weapons!" he'd shouted. "Why aren't you people providing them?"

"Money's tight and the government's position is precarious."

"What about us? And the people whose homes have been destroyed?"

"I'm well aware of that. We all are. Be patient. We'll do everything we can."

"Or is it enough for you just to watch?" What fury! Just like fire.

But what was going on in Cairo?

There was no car to take him anywhere. In the station square, people were walking in every direction, anger on their faces, heaping curses on the British. It was cold. The sky was hidden by ominous clouds; the wind was still and lifeless. Shops were closed as if for mourning, and thick smoke rose along on the skyline.

What was going on in Cairo?

Cautiously, he began to walk, then beckoned to a man coming toward him. "What's going on in town?" he asked.

"The last day's come," was the bewildered reply.

"What do you mean? Protest demonstrations?"

"Fire and destruction," the man yelled, moving on.

As he started walking again, slowly and cautiously, looking carefully at what was going on around him, he asked himself in bewilderment where the police and the Army were.

In Sharia Ibrahim, things looked even worse and showed clearly what was really happening: the whole square had been given over to angry people. Feelings from the depths of their subconscious had erupted like a volcano and they were shrieking, howling like dogs. Anyone standing on either side was seized; gasoline was flowing, fires were burning, doors were being knocked in, all kinds of merchandise was being strewn about, and water was gushing out in clashing waves. This insanity, uncontrolled, was Cairo in revolt, but revolting against itself, bringing on itself the very thing it wanted to bring on its enemies. It was suicide. And he asked himself in dismay what could be behind it all.

His instinct warned him of grave danger in the future. Tomorrow the true extent of the tragedy would become clear, and with it a real danger, threatening the very essence of our lives—threatening us, not the British, threatening Cairo, the course of battle at the Canal, and the stability of the government. Threatening him too in that he was considered a part of that government. This flood would uproot the government, the party, and himself. It was no good trying to squeeze the fear out of his mind or pretending—in the face of this swirling spirit of unreason that engulfed him on all sides, more powerful than madness, destruction, and fire— pretending to forget it. He trusted this instinct of his implicitly; it had been his harbinger in times of political crisis, warning him time after time on the eve of all those occasions when his party had been dismissed from office. Perhaps this was the end. If so, it would be a fatal one. And there would have been nothing like it before.

Feeling utterly bewildered, he kept walking toward the center of the city. He decided to find out all he could. After all, he was a responsible person, and even though his position was a minor one, relatively speaking, he was still responsible and should see everything for himself.

The din was unbearable, as though every atom on earth were yelling at once. Flames were spreading everywhere, dancing in windows, crackling on roofs, licking at walls, and flying up into the smoke that hung where the sky should have been. The burning smelled hellish, a concoction of wood, clothes, and different kinds of oil. Stifled cries could be heard coming out of the smoke. Young men and boys, in frenzied unconcern, were destroying everything, and walls kept collapsing with a rumble like thunder. Concealed anger, suppressed despair, unreleased tension, all the things people had been nursing inside them, had suddenly burst their bottle, exploding like some hurricane of demons.

Many things should be burned, he told himself, but not Cairo. You people don't know what you're doing. A whole division of British troops couldn't do a tenth of the damage you're doing here. The battle at the Canal is over. We lost. I've been through hardships before and my heart doesn't lie to me. The government has no soldiers and the fire is raging out of control. Is it to be allowed to consume this whole great city? Are three million people going to spend the night without any shelter? Are destruction, disease, and chaos going to spread, until the British come back to restore order again? Have people put aside independence, nationalism, and their greater aspirations merely to go through this ordeal of destruction? Creeping into his heart like an ant came a sense of despair and the world momentarily went black before his eyes, and his confidence disappeared.

Men on the street corners urged people on. "Burn! Destroy! Long live the homeland!" they yelled.

He looked at them with curious resentment and would have liked to be able to stop them, but the buffeting stream of people made it impossible even to pause. They were unknown faces to him; not from his party or any other, strangers, who seemed to exude the smell of treason, of which he imagined a putrid reek in the air even more gloomy than the smoke itself. Disconsolate and at a loss, he gave an angry sigh.

"Burn! Destroy! Long live the homeland!"

Miserable wretches! Had all that blood been wasted at the Canal? What about the dead policemen and their officers? Everything valuable, everything worthwhile, was going up in smoke. How could he get to the ministry and find the people in charge? The streets were full of smashed cars; the sky had turned a deep red color as the fires blazed away under their black cloud of smoke. What would the furious commando have to say if he could see this bloody spectacle of treason? What would he say if he could hear these shouts?

"Burn! Destroy! Long live the homeland!"

Fire, destruction, and smoke, the awful hallmarks of the day, made even worse by the air of conspiracy that lurked on street corners. Waves of berserk demonstrators kept crashing into him as if they didn't see him in his long gray coat. Swallowing hard, he said nothing, though he lost his balance, and the briefcase he was clutching knocked against his leg. All the details of the report he had to submit to the minister, describing the way the battle had gone and the commandos' requests, had gone right out of his mind and he thought only about the future, which seemed to loom before his eyes like the smoke of the city burning. Heading toward a street where things seemed calmer and more quiet, he recalled the comment of a shaikh who was a member of Parliament on the subject of the annulment of the treaty, "It's the end for us," he'd said. "Now things are in God's hands."

He'd been sitting next to the shaikh at the club and had lost his temper at the time. "That's how you people in Parliament are," he had yelled. "You only care about your own interests!"

"This is the end," the shaikh had repeated with great emphasis, in a tone of voice not entirely devoid of irony. "Now it is in God's hands."

"In our entire glorious past," he had said enthusiastically, "there's never been a situation like this one!"

The shaikh had toyed with his mustache. "Oh yes there was," he had replied sadly. "Saad's* time, for example. But it's the end now!"

A seasoned old man might be justified in having put the

---

*An asterisk indicates that the name or term so denoted is explained in the Notes section at the end of the book.

age of enthusiasm behind him. But here was Cairo burning. And these traitors standing on the street corners—there were so many of them! Everything was quite obvious, but there was so little that could be done about it that the best plan seemed to be to get drunk on a cocktail of woes, to wallow in it until you drowned. The sky itself was strewn with blackened splinters from all the destruction, and a sense of grief seemed to materialize out of it as palpably as from an animal's dead carcass.

He felt tired and decided to head for home, imagining that, tortoiselike, he would have to spend a long time on the road before glimpsing the high parts of Dokki.

TWO

Later, at nightfall, he went to Shukri Pasha* Abd al-Halim's palatial house, a quarter of an hour away from his own home in Dokki.* The Pasha received him in his study and they sat down facing each other. The Pasha's stubby form seemed almost lost in the big chair and his small, round, smooth-skinned face showed gloom wrapped in the tranquillity of old age. His gray English suit was extremely smart and he wore a red tarboosh on his babylike bald head. The greetings they exchanged were cursory, a sign of the critical nature of the situation. Isa felt awkward at first: the Pasha had had his eye on the ministerial position, but for a month or more Isa himself had hesitated about putting his name forward for the first cabinet reshuffle; and wondered what this old man would be thinking. He'd waited so long for a ministry. But the Pasha's energies for office work had sunk to their lowest ebb and he no longer had any real job except to serve on the Finance Committee in Parliament. Isa felt as sorry for him as he did for himself and looked at him diffidently, as though it were a kind of consolation. After a rest at home some of Isa's color had returned and he felt better as he sat there in the chair, while the Pasha kept turning the wedding ring on his finger. The worst kind of loss was one that affected both private and public life at the same time.

"We'll be dating things from today for a long time to come," the Pasha said.

"I saw some of it myself," Isa said, eager to hear any news. "What a black day!" He lowered his head—which looked large and elongated in the mirror across the room—until his black wavy hair came close to the Pasha's eyes. Then, frowning, he lifted it again so that he could look straight at the Pasha.

"So Cairo was burning when you came in?"

"Yes, Pasha. It was pure hell."

"How terrible! What were things like over at the Canal?"

"The young men were all full of enthusiasm, but they need weapons desperately. The massacre of the policemen shattered everyone."

"That was a criminal affair. A disaster."

"Yes," Isa replied angrily. "We're being pushed toward—" The rest of his sentence needed no saying and his words faded away. Their eyes met sadly.

"What are people saying about us?" the Pasha asked.

"Nationalist feelings are running very high. Our enemies are saying that we manufactured a battle to take people's minds off us." He lowered the corner of his mouth in contempt. "They'll always find something to say," he went on. "Miserable wretches—scoundrels!"

Between them was a table with a silver jug and a tray of biscuits on it. The Pasha motioned to Isa to pour out two glasses and they proceeded to drink although neither of them enjoyed it. During all this, Isa looked around at the picture of Saad Zaghlul* hanging on the wall above the huge desk to the right of where they were sitting.

"Would you believe, sir, that I haven't been able to contact my minister so far?" Isa asked.

The Pasha quietly stroked his silver-gray mustache. "I can't blame you for complaining these days," he said. "Where's the minister? No one knows. Where's the Army? No one knows. Where are the police? No one knows. The public security system has disappeared and meanwhile the devil's on a rampage."

"I wonder if the fire's still burning."

The Pasha stretched his legs till they reached around one of the ebony legs of the table. His black shoes shone more brightly in the gleam of the quadrangular crystal chandelier. Isa glanced at the heater mounted on the wall and was struck by the transparency of the flickering red flame; it made him think of the Magi and he began to enjoy the pleasant warmth it was giving out. His eyes glided over the classical-style furniture, which seemed to be shrouded in a kind of dignity and antique splendor, and at the same time to convey the sorrow of departure, which in turn made him think of Antony's funeral speech over the body of Caesar.

"The fire should be out by now," Shukri Pasha Abd al-Halim replied with careful indifference. "That is, now that it has done its job!"

The young man's honey-brown eyes gleamed. He tried to draw some more out of the Pasha. "Maybe it was just reckless anger," he suggested tentatively.

The Pasha showed his teeth as he smiled. "It was anger all right!" he replied. "But beyond that anger there was envy. Anger may be genuinely reckless, but envy always follows a distinct plan of action."

"How can this happen when we're in power?"

The Pasha gave a dry and abrupt laugh. "Today's like an overcast night," he replied. "Wait till we find out where the head and feet are."

Isa breathed in sharply and then sighed so hard that the fringe of the velvet tablecloth rustled. "What about the parties?" he muttered.

"They're too weak to organize anything at all!" the Pasha replied, both corners of his mouth curving down as a sign of contempt.

"Who then?" asked Isa with a clear look of doubt in his eyes.

"Things are not as obvious as you imagine," the Pasha replied. "It is possible that prearranged signals filtered through from the Palace; it is also possible that English spies are in high spirits over the havoc they have caused. But it seems to me that this deluge began quite naturally and then certain people took advantage of the situation."

Suddenly deep-seated anxieties stirred inside Isa's mind and his heart jumped. "But what about the battle?" he asked.

The Pasha slowly twisted his mustache and looked up at the ceiling, where lights hidden behind golden wings were gleaming in the four corners. Then he looked at the young man again, his eyes showing all the signs of his own uncertainty and depression without needing to say a word.

"Damn anyone who let's himself get talked into trifling with our struggle!" said Isa, trying to fend off his own apprehension.

No signs of cheerful optimism appeared on the Pasha's face. He simply made do with replying, "Today will have grave consequences."

"For the second time today," said Isa, suddenly feeling listless and defeated, "I'm reminded of what Shaikh Abd at-Tawwab as-Salhubi said after the annulment of the treaty: 'It's the end for us. Now it's in God's hands.' "

The Pasha smiled. "It'll never be the end for us," he said. "We may fall but we'll come back even more powerful than before."

The telephone rang. It was the Pasha's wife calling from the top floor. He looked upset as he put the receiver back in its cradle.

"Martial law's been declared," he said.

They both sat for a while astonished, then Isa broke the silence. "Perhaps it's necessary," he muttered, "so that they can arrest the culprits." But then he noticed that the Pasha was lost in his own morose thoughts, and tried to make amends. "Martial law in our times!" he said. "What a terrible thing to happen!"

"It was not declared because of our times," the Pasha replied, frowning.

THREE

"A decree's been issued transferring me from my position in the minister's office to the archives."

His mother raised her head and looked at him. Her thin face was much like his own, especially in its triangular shape, but heavily wrinkled, with signs of age in her eyes, mouth, and jaw.

"It's not the first time," she said. "Don't worry, you'll get your old job back. Or maybe something even better. Our Lord will put things right."

The sitting room overlooked Sharia Halim in Dokki. The wide window of the balcony was closed as a protection against the cold and behind it willow branches rose and fell limply. Beyond them clouds stretched away into the distance, bunched together, foreboding. Like the political situation. The ministry had been dismissed, and the new minister had removed him from his job, along with many other people, especially anyone who had been connected with the battle at the Canal. But these things had happened so often that his mother had come to regard them as almost normal. She had become quite used to seeing the most disastrous floods followed by a smooth ebb, which always turned out to be in the best interests of her beloved son. Though old and illiterate, she still followed current events closely and kept up with whatever was going on in politics, especially with matters that affected Isa's life.

She was very proud of him and believed everything he said. His success amazed her—it was so far beyond anything she had ever imagined—it had been beyond the hopes of either her or his late father, who had spent his entire life as an obscure minor civil servant. In spite of the pitfalls and storms of politics, Isa had forged ahead, floundering at times to such an extent that people gave him up for lost, but then always rising again to achieve some new level of seniority. This gorgeous house in Dokki was a sign of his successful ambition, and its furniture was a delight to behold. Pashas and ministers would frequently favor him with visits.

His mother held a rosary from the Hijaz* in her gnarled hands and used the beads in litanies to God. Would there be an end to this situation, she asked herself, and would everything turn out for the best? Were there complicated factors involved which were difficult to comprehend or was it just that the evil eye had struck?

"It's incredible," said Isa listlessly, "that we have hardly settled into the business of running the government for a year before we're thrown out again for four. We're the legitimate rulers of this country and there are no others besides us."

"Health and well-being are the important things," the old lady said with firm conviction.

He smiled bitterly, but concealed his real feelings. "I think it's important," he said, "that I take advantage of this period of retirement to attend to my personal affairs."

Her dim eyes flickered with interest and for the first time she spoke joyfully: "Oh, I'm delighted. It's about time you got married. The girl is waiting for you and her father has not withheld his consent."

"Wouldn't it be better," he asked with a laugh, "to get married when I'm enjoying a prestigious position in authority?"

She smiled and her teeth gleamed, like some forgotten sprig of jasmine in a garden where all the trees have been uprooted. "You've got a prestigious position now," she said. "People realize that you've been nominated for senior posts.

Ali Bey* Sulaiman understands these things very well. And besides, he's your relative. He loved your late father more than anything else in the world."

All this was true. Ali Bey Sulaiman was his father's cousin, on a side of the family tree that was otherwise bare. Rich and from a rich background, he was also an influential justice, quite apart from the fact that he was a Palace man. Once Isa strengthened his position by becoming the Bey's son-in-law, he would be able to depend upon his father-in-law for a convenient harbor to shelter in whenever his boat was rocked by political storms—an important consideration since the losses he would suffer from remaining with the party seemed likely to outlast any possible gains. And besides, Salwa was really a marvelous girl. There was no comparison between her and his other cousin, whose family had been trying for ages to get him to marry her. Salwa's mother was a fine woman too; she tended to a conservatism rare among people of her class. Fortunately for Isa, she thought very well of his future prospects, to such an extent that she could envisage him as a minister even before he himself could: when he had broached the subject of asking for her daughter's hand, she had told him quite frankly that she was not interested in money but in status. And wasn't the second grade* a real sign of distinction for a young man in his thirties? She had a particular admiration for young men who had studied abroad, and even though he had not done so himself, he had still served for a year in the London embassy and traveled as an attaché with the secretariat of the delegation to the treaty negotiations. He liked to visualize Salwa's enticing beauty, her crème-Chantilly complexion. It was just as well for him that she was not a socialite, one of those girls who went to clubs or had taken up modern ideas.

"Do you realize," he asked his mother, "that I hadn't seen her since we were children?"

"That's your fault!" his mother retorted. "The fact that you were so involved in your work is no excuse either. Anyone with a relative like Ali Bey Sulaiman should have kept in as close contact as possible."

"I used to meet him abroad, but I wasn't thinking of marriage at that time."

When he'd asked her father for her hand he'd had only the vaguest picture in his mind of what she actually looked like. But he'd found her to be a real gem and had fallen in love with her with all his heart. He was in the process of choosing the appropriate words to express his new feelings to his mother when Umm Shalabi came in to announce that his cousin Hasan had come to pay him a visit. Still nursing defeat, Isa felt unready for this particular caller, and so it was annoyance that predominated over his other feelings.

Hasan Ali ad-Dabbagh came in beaming. Of medium height, well built, with a square face and deep-lined features, he had a broad chin, and his clear intelligent eyes and sharp-pointed nose were very distinctive. He kissed his aunt's hand, shook Isa's warmly without managing to lessen the latter's feelings of annoyance, then sat down beside him and asked for some tea. He was almost the same age as Isa but was still in the fifth grade, whereas politics had managed to push Isa up to the second. Though he had a bachelor's degree in commerce, the only work he'd been able to find was with the draft board.

"How are you?" Isa's mother asked.

"I'm fine," Hasan replied, "and my mother and sister are well too."

Isa felt even more uncomfortable at the mention of his sister; not because he disliked her but because she was the sister of this old rival of his. They'd been competitors, in close contact, and had once harbored harsh and painful sentiments against each other. It was only politics that had put an end to the causes of this contentiousness between the two of them: politics had raised Isa to his important position, while merely nudging Hasan on in slow stages down a long, arduous road. Their relationship had flagged somewhat, but feelings ran very deep, and Hasan had never cut himself off from his cousin completely. Hasan even wanted Isa to marry his sister and, amazingly enough, had let it be known that he seriously contemplated going to see Ali Bey Sulaiman to ask for his daughter's hand only a few days after Isa had done so himself. Isa had laughed in scorn when he'd heard the news and told himself that God should have some mercy on a man who knows his own worth. Nevertheless, even though he disliked Hasan, Isa still reserved a certain admiration for him on account of his strong personality and considerable intelligence.

"I heard you've been transferred to the archives," Hasan said. "Don't worry," he continued generously, "you're someone who was made to stand up to hardships."

Isa's mother entered the conversation. "There's nothing to be worried about," she said enthusiastically, "that's what I always say. Why do these people abandon their leaders and then take vengeance on their sons?"

Isa was a little nonplussed by Hasan's sympathy. "We're quite used to being imprisoned and beaten," he said proudly. "Today's afflictions are nothing . . ."

Hasan smiled and went on sipping his tea. "That's right," he said with traces of aggression in his voice, "you're imprisoned and beaten while the other people do a little bargaining."

Isa realized full well whom he meant by "other people" and got ready for battle, while his mother left the room to perform the sunset prayer. "You know very well what I think of the others personally," he said by way of warning, "so be careful!"

"Everything's collapsing so fast," said Hasan with a provocative grin. "It's best to let it happen. The old way of doing things must be torn up by the roots!"

"And what about the problems our nation faces?" Isa retorted. "Who'll be left to deal with them?"

"Do you think that those corrupt idiots in Parliament are the ones to solve them?"

"You don't see them as they really are."

"The truth is that I *do* see them as they really are."

"You keep on repeating exactly the things that the opposition press is saying!"

"I only believe in the truth," Hasan replied with a confidence that was exasperating. "Young people have to rely on themselves."

Isa stifled his own irritation. "A call for total destruction is very dangerous," he said. "If it weren't for this treachery, we could have kept the King within his constitutional limits and got our independence."

Hasan finished his glass and smiled, trying to clear the atmosphere. "You're a loyal man," he said amiably, "and that leads you to respect certain people who don't deserve it. There's widespread corruption, believe me. Nobody in a position of authority today thinks about anything but the rotten game of getting rich quick. We inhale corruption in the very air we breathe! How can any of our genuine hopes emerge from this quagmire?"

They could both hear the sound of Isa's mother praying. For the sake of hospitality, Isa controlled his temper. Nothing could make him admit that what his rival was saying was right: sheer obstinacy would hold him back. But he felt extremely depressed: the world was changing and his gods were crumbling before his very eyes. For his part, Hasan changed the subject and began talking about the property lost in the fire, the estimates of compensation, the position of the

British, and the continual arrests. Before long, however, he came back to the point: "Just show me a single sector that doesn't ooze with corruption!"

What appalling notions! How impudent and thoroughly irritating he was! Just then, Isa remembered a totally unconnected event that had happened a long time ago. He had gone to visit Ali Bey Sulaiman's house with his father and found himself alone in the dining room, where he'd noticed a piece of chocolate in a half-opened drawer. He had slipped in his hand and taken it. That had happened almost a quarter of a century ago. What a memory! As always, Hasan kept up his attack—damn him!

"What is it you want?" Isa asked listlessly.

"Fresh clean blood."

"Where from?"

Hasan's pearly teeth gleamed as he laughed with health and well-being. "The country's not dead yet," he said.

"Show me a group of people apart from our party that deserves any confidence!" Isa demanded angrily.

Hasan glared back at him without saying a word. Outside, the old lady's voice could be heard in a flow of prayers.

"What's to be done then?" Isa resumed.

"We'll support the devil himself if he volunteers to save the ship."

"But the devil won't volunteer to save anything." Isa glared away, looking unconcernedly up at the pitch-black sky, trying to avoid Hasan's gaze for a while.

"The English, the King, and the parties, they'll all have to go," Hasan said. "Then we must start afresh."

Isa laughed bitterly. "The burning of Cairo has made it clear that treason is more powerful than the government and the people put together," he said.

His mother came back into the room. "Isn't there something else you can talk about?" she asked. Her cheeks looked flushed and puffy as she sat down in her old seat. "When are you going to get married?" she asked Hasan.

At that point Isa was reminded of Hasan's bold attempt to get engaged to Salwa and that made him even more annoyed. Hasan was poor but brash. It was obvious he was after her money, as a final way of getting himself out of his difficulties.

"Momentous events are happening so suddenly," Hasan replied with a laugh, "and without the slightest warning."

"When will you be seeing your mother to give her our greetings?"

"Your house is a long way from Rod al-Farag, but she'll definitely be coming to visit you." Hasan was on the point of standing up to leave. "Where are you going this evening?" he asked Isa.

"To the club," Isa replied defiantly but calmly.

Hasan got up. "Goodbye," he said, "till we meet again!"

FOUR

The day the engagement was announced at Ali Bey Sulaiman's mansion was one to remember. Men and women were
not really separated from each other; they occupied two
drawing rooms connected by a common entrance which was
considered a beautiful work of art in its own right. Isa's
mother and her sister-in-law, Hasan's mother, were sitting
among the female guests in the red room, while Isa's close
friends, Samir Abd al-Baqi, Abbas Sadiq, Ibrahim Khairat,
and his cousin Hasan, were all sitting in the green room
among the family guests and relatives. The important guests
were being welcomed in the large room adjoining the entrance. These included Ali Bey Sulaiman's friends, all of them
Palace men or people connected with the law, and party men
who were acquaintances of Isa. Isa's mother and her sister-
in-law withdrew into themselves as they sat there in the glare
of the brilliant lights which were shining down on them. Neither of them seemed to have any connection with the world
around her. Isa's mother was wearing an expensive dress and
her age gave her a certain dignity. Her senses were weak—
especially her sight and hearing—and this made her less re-
ceptive to the festive atmosphere. She withdrew into herself
and made no effort to give any kind of impression that might
be considered appropriate for the future groom's mother.

Susan Hanem,* Ali Bey Sulaiman's wife, made a special
effort to be nice to her so as to make her feel more at home.
She had been fond of Isa's mother for a long time—at least
since she had become Ali Bey Sulaiman's wife—and her affection for the old lady had been one of the reasons that had

led her to agree to accept Isa as a future son-in-law. A chronic liver disease and a bad kidney condition had left Susan Hanem in her mid-fifties with only her height, proportions, and immutable grace to mark what had once been great beauty. "Don't forget you're in your own home," she told Isa's mother very kindly.

Hasan started a fierce argument about politics with Isa's friends even though he did not know them well. Isa listened to him for a while from a distance. He had thought that Hasan would not come to the reception and his behavior astonished him. Hasan could defy time itself if he wanted, Isa was convinced of that.

But Isa did not stay in one place for long, giving particular attention to his guests from the party. The atmosphere in the room was a little tense. The party men were all facing the Palace men, but even though they were bound together by old ties of friendship, the majority of each group was pretending not to know the other. In all this, Ali Bey Sulaiman was playing his role with unerring skill. He was greeting everyone on equal terms even though he was a Palace man himself. He had been an ordinary lawyer until the Palace had nominated him for the post of justice in one of the judicial reshuffles. Not recognized as having any particular political coloring, he had become a kind of political rainbow, then, just at the right moment, had joined the Unity Party, becoming attached to the King's retinue, from which he had risen to occupy the highest position in the judiciary. Though he was nearly sixty, he still enjoyed extraordinary good health and vigor. He was tall and had a marvelous athletic posture and his black eyes, which gleamed beneath bushy eyebrows, made him irresistibly attractive. Very early in his life he had given himself the valuable support of marrying into the Himmat family—Susan Hanem's family—and had then laid out his patch of earth and planted the aristocracy in his progeny.

He started laughing and joking with all his guests. "Happy occasions should bring together people who disagree about politics!" he said.

"Do you think," Shukri Pasha Abd al-Halim whispered in Isa's ear, "that your relative is acknowledging by that joke that the King's men—and consequently the King himself—aren't above the parties?"

Shaikh Abd as-Sattar as-Salhubi leaned over in their direction to hear what they were whispering and then laughed silently. "In that case," he whispered in turn, "the parties should be above the King!" He then looked anxiously at the picture of the King hanging on the central wall of the room.

Isa smiled. "Don't worry," he said. "People are heaping curses on him quite openly in cafés."

But as the party and the drinks proceeded, the bitterness of politics vanished. Even Isa, who was a political creature above all else, abandoned himself wholeheartedly to his feelings of sheer joy. He knew that he was immaculately dressed, that there was a glow on his triangular face, and that his round eyes looked serene and limpid. The happiness he felt at the thought of marrying into a wealthy and influential family was a mere trifle compared with his feelings about his bride-to-be and his sincere hopes for a really pleasant life, for a tomorrow packed with happiness, a future which would hold the promise of real prestige. He forgot about the burning of Cairo, his dismissal from the ministry and transfer to the archives, the depressing apathy that had dampened popular enthusiasm, the indolence that seemed to be endemic in official quarters, and the gloomy melancholy that, even while the glories of spring were giving physical life an intoxicating stimulus, tinged the horizon.

In his present excited state, Isa did not have to stay in one spot any longer than suited him. He went over to Susan Hanem and they took a final look at the buffet together; everything seemed to be there and it all looked very colorful. Then he made for the green room and sat down with his closest friends, where he would have liked to stay until he was called for the announcement of the engagement. Ibrahim Khairat was looking into the red room. "There's a whole lot of white flesh in there," he said. "It looks beautiful!"

"Do you mean Al-Hajja,* Isa's mother?" Abbas Sadiq asked jokingly.

Isa looked at his mother in her expensive but modest gown and was happy that she looked more dignified than Hasan's mother in spite of the latter's beauty. Abbas Sadiq started to complain to him about Hasan. "Your cousin's fiercer than the Cairo fire itself!" he said. Hasan gave a long laugh and Abbas carried on in a cautionary tone. "Get married yourself and you'll be convinced that it isn't all that bad to belong to a party."

"Things are very confused at the moment," Samir Abd al-Baqi interjected.

They all realized that it was politics he was talking about.

"There's no question about that," Isa replied.

"But they're even more confused than is generally apparent," said Samir emphatically.

"May the good Lord honor you!" Hasan said sarcastically.

"They say the King is going to hire mercenaries. Because he doesn't trust anyone any longer!"

"Nothing shows more clearly how bad things are," Abbas Sadiq commented with a laugh, "than what one of the Liberal Constitutionalists said. He declared he'd rather have the Wafd* return to power than put up with the present chaotic state of affairs."

"May God increase the confusion and chaos!" Hasan replied with great emphasis.

Isa was called inside for the announcement of the engagement. Everyone was watching him and there was complete silence; for Hasan it was a very heavy silence. Then the shrill cries of joy echoing through every part of the mansion pierced the air.

Salwa stood with her mother on one side and Isa on the other. Then she walked around among the guests before taking her seat in the red room on a chair banked with roses. She looked really beautiful. She had inherited her mother's stature and long, thin neck, and had her father's eyes set in a face that seemed to have a white translucence like moonlight, but with a sweet gentle expression that showed not only a kindly temperament but also an almost total lack of intelligence or warmth. She looked at her mother continually, as if asking her guidance and help, fearful and insecure at the thought of separation. The guests discussed her dress at length.

As the party continued, the piles of food prepared for the buffet disappeared and guests started to leave, carrying souvenir tins of sweets with them. The engaged couple and Susan Hanem were finally left alone in the sitting room. Its huge veranda looked out onto Baron Street. Night was spreading through the pure spring air, and the full-grown trees around the garden, swimming in the brilliance of the electric lights, swayed from side to side in the gentle breeze, moist with refreshing coolness.

"Today I think I've reached the peak of happiness," Isa said.

"Thank you!" Salwa whispered with a bashful smile. "I hope I can tell you how I feel—when I find enough courage."

Susan Hanem watched them both happily. "When you are married in July, God willing," she said, "our happiness will be complete."

Isa wondered when he would be allowed to kiss Salwa. He was so drunk with happiness that it almost worried him. He would follow in Ali Bey's footsteps, he told himself, and eventually come to occupy the same kind of position. He had never tasted the feeling of love before, except once when he was in secondary school. He'd fallen in love with a nurse at the morning tram stop, and had plunged into the experience headlong—foolishly—but his father had eventually brought him under control again. Now here he was today, having gone through imprisonment, beatings, dismissal, promotion, and demotion, here he was engaged to a fiancée whom he hadn't seen in more than ten years. Now, he knew about love and had already drunk from its nectar. He felt almost as if he was clutching guaranteed happiness with his hands. "You're the image of your mother, my beloved," he said, "so dazzling I can't conceive how happy I really am."

Susan Hanem laughed. "I hope you'll remember what you've just said in the future," she said. "People say that we mothers-in-law get to hear nice things like that only on this one occasion!"

Salwa gave a gentle laugh and Isa felt even happier. Suddenly he felt the urge to show off. "I wonder if you'll dislike living abroad," he asked, "if circumstances make it necessary in the future to work in the diplomatic service?"

"Salwa graduated from a German school," Susan Hanem replied for her daughter.

He smiled to show how pleased he was. "Let's hope our life will be happy," he murmured. "We've seen real suffering and I hope our happiness will be real too."

FIVE

"There's a secret in our life," Isa told Salwa, "which you ought to know." They were sitting together on the veranda, the scent of roses and carnations all around them. It was almost sunset; daylight had half-closed its eyelids and the sun was withdrawing its lashes from the mansion rooftops. Spring seemed to be breathing with the pure energy of youth. Susan Hanem had disappeared for a while and left them alone. They were drinking lemonade. A crystal decanter stood on a table of painted rattan.

"A secret?" Salwa whispered inquisitively.

He lifted himself, beginning with his eyebrows, something he always did when he was on the point of speaking. "Yes," he said. "You may think that I hadn't seen you before when I asked for your hand. But in fact I loved you tremendously ten years ago; you were ten and I was twenty. We were living in my mother's house in Al-Wayiliyya* and your family lived out by the Pyramids. Your father was a lawyer in those days and a close friend of my father and they used to visit each other a lot. You were very beautiful then, as you are now, and I fell in love with you. Don't you remember those days?"

She stifled a laugh by biting the inside of her lip. "Only a little," she replied. "I remember seeing rockets on the Prophet's birthday at your house once, but I don't remember anything about your loving me . . ."

He laughed, tossing his head back in a particular way, quite unwittingly copying one of the pashas in the party.

"No one remembers such things," he said. "But my late

42

father had to restrain me once when I was looking at you in utter infatuation and on another occasion when I kissed you!"

"No!"

"Yes! A pure kiss to match your tender age."

"But you weren't a child."

"No, but you were! It doesn't matter anyway. Work hard and you'll marry her, my father told me at the time; make sure you turn out to be a young man who is worthy of her and I'll see you're married! I asked what degree of worthiness was required, and my father replied that Ali Bey Sulaiman was his relative and close friend but we needed Susan Hanem's approval. She was rich and not concerned with wealth; what she wanted for her daughter was a successful young man—a judge, for example. The fact of the matter is that my own rapid promotion has impressed a number of people. I've become an important civil servant—no, politician even—at a very early age. But no one knew what the real reasons were for this unusual energy on my part!"

With a graceful gesture, she opened an ivory fan. On its outer edge was a picture of a swimming duck. "All this, and yet you hadn't been to see me for ten years!" she said with mild irony.

"Don't forget," he said earnestly, "that your father was appointed a justice after that, that he worked for years plying between Asyut and Alexandria, and that I myself got heavily involved in politics."

"How were you to know that ten years hadn't turned me into something awful?" she asked with a coquettish smile.

"My heart! I trust its feelings. And when I saw you again my confidence in it was doubled. So our betrothal may seem traditional on the surface, but there's a real love story behind it even though it was all one-sided."

"Well, at any rate," she murmured, gazing into the distance, "it's not that way any longer."

He took her chin between his fingers, turned her head gently, leaned forward until his hungry mouth met her soft lips in a throbbing kiss, then drew his head back again, smiling with a sense of happiness so deep that as his eyes wandered over the collection of flowerpots on the veranda, they were misted with emotion like a fog-covered windowpane. The tale he'd told her was not a complete fabrication. Not all along the line, in any case. He had often admired her beauty in the past and he really loved her now, even if he'd forgotten her for ten years. So what harm was there in a little white lie, which was a shining example of good sense and which would give their relationship a magical beauty of its own?

His beloved was not ready, however, to be parted from her mother; it was almost as though the midwife had forgotten to sever the umbilical cord. This attachment worried him sometimes. He looked forward eagerly to the day when he would really have her completely as his own and was somewhat disturbed by the way she looked at her mother during breaks in conversation. But his happiness swept all misgivings away, just as a big wave will sweep away the flotsam from a beach and leave it smooth and clean, and he found delight in the fact that she had so appallingly little experience of life's normal happenings. Her innocence may in fact have flattered his own feelings by simply giving him a sense of superiority. He was also pleased at her love of music and her wide reading of travel literature.

"For me your love is a treasure without price," he said. "When I came to meet you for the first time, I asked God that I might make a good impression on you."

"I'd seen you before in the newspapers."

"If I'd known that at the time, I'd have taken more care getting ready for the photograph!" he replied delightedly.

"That doesn't matter. But I also heard about your misfortunes in politics."

As he laughed, he threw his head back once again like the pasha. "I wonder what you make of that?" he asked. "I'm an old friend of police truncheons and prison cells. I'm quite used to being dismissed and expelled. What do you think of that?"

She bit the inside of her lip once more. "Papa says . . ."

"There's no need to quote Papa on the subject," he interrupted quickly. "I know what he thinks already; he belongs to the other side. But don't you think about anything but music and travel books? From now on, you're going to have to prepare yourself for the role of a politician's wife—a politician in every sense of the word."

Susan Hanem came back into the room. "Everything is as you wish," she said, sounding like someone announcing that a project had been successfully concluded.

"Thank you, madame," Isa replied, standing there in his sharkskin suit. They both sat down. "The marriage will be in August, then," he continued, smoothing his trousers over his knees, "and afterwards we'll travel directly to Europe."

Their eyes met in delight. The last ray of the sun had disappeared. "I was telling Salwa that I've loved her for ten years!" he told Susan Hanem.

The lady raised her eyebrows in surprise. "Don't believe everything he tells you," she warned her daughter. "Your fiancé is a politician and I know all about these politicians!"

All three of them dissolved in laughter.

SIX

Isa was at breakfast on the morning of the twenty-third of July* when the radio interrupted its normal broadcast to announce the Army declaration. At first he did not fully comprehend what he was hearing. Then he leapt up and stared at the radio, listening dry-mouthed to these strange words which kept following each other, forming startling sentences. When he realized what he was hearing, his immediate reaction was dismay. He reeled, like someone suddenly coming out of darkness into brilliant light. What could it all mean?

He went into the sitting room and sat down next to his mother. "Very grave news," he said.

She raised her dim eyes in his direction.

"The Army's defying the King!" he said.

She found the news hard to digest. "Is it like the days of Urabi Pasha?"* she asked.

Ah! Why had that thought not occurred to him? He was really in a very agitated state. "Yes," he muttered, "like the days of Urabi."

"Will there be war?" she asked anxiously.

What would really happen? He couldn't get any more news now since there was no one left in Cairo to consult. The only reason why he himself was not on vacation was that he'd postponed it until the time for his trip abroad.

"No, no," he told his mother, "the Army's making some demands and they'll be met. That's all there is to it."

He traveled to Alexandria, mulling over what had happened en route. Here was the tyrant himself being dealt a blow of steel: it should match the brutality of his own tyranny and should be final—let him burn, in the contemplation of his own crimes. Just look at the consequences of your errors and stupidity! But where would this movement stop? What would be the party's role in it? At one moment, Isa would feel intoxicated by a sense of hope; at others, he would be overcome by a feeling much like the whimpering uneasiness dogs show immediately before an earthquake.

He found Abd al-Halim Pasha in Athenios* wearing a white suit of natural silk with a deep red rose in the buttonhole of the jacket. In the glass on the table in front of him, all that was left was the froth of a bottle of stout, looking as though it was stained with iodine. The Pasha narrowed his eyes languorously. "Forget about the Army's demands," he said. "The movement's bigger than that. The demands can be met today and the people who are putting them forward will hang tomorrow. No, no, my dear sir! But it's very difficult to judge what's behind it all."

"Haven't you any news, sir?"

"Things are moving too fast for news. Godwin, the English journalist, was sitting where you are just an hour ago, and he assured me that the King's finished."

The shock was tremendous. It overwhelmed him for a moment. "Don't we have any connection with what's going on?" he asked.

"One can't be sure about anything. Who are these officers? And don't forget that our leaders are abroad."

"Maybe their journey abroad has got something to do with the movement?" Isa suggested.

The Pasha's expression showed no signs of optimism. His only comment was a barely audible "Maybe."

They continued their conversation without saying anything new; this became an end in itself, providing a release for their anxieties.

He found Ali Bey Sulaiman in his villa at Sidi Bishr,* sitting in a bamboo rocking chair, his forehead contracted into a frown and looking haggard and sickly, all healthy good looks and innate haughtiness gone. When he looked up and saw Isa approaching, he gave him an anxious stare. "What news have you got?" he asked impatiently.

Isa sat down. He could feel the burden as the Bey, his wife, and his daughter looked at him. As he spoke, there was a superficial calm to his voice, concealing a certain pride at the new factor he was about to introduce to the situation. "The King's finished," he said.

The last gleam went out of the Bey's eyes. He threw a sickly glance through the balcony toward the pounding sea. "What about you? I mean you people. Do you approve?"

For a moment Isa enjoyed a sense of exultation, a moment that seemed itself to swing to and fro above a painful wound. "The King's our traditional enemy," he mumbled.

The Bey sat up straight in his chair. "Has the party got anything to do with what's happening?" he asked.

Isa would have loved to be able to give an affirmative answer to these people who were looking at him. "I don't have any information about that," he replied, concealing his own chagrin.

"But you can find out, no doubt."

"No one whom I've met knows anything. Our leaders are abroad, as you know, sir."

The Bey snorted angrily. "We've forgotten the lesson of the Urabi revolt pretty quickly," he said. "The British will be marching in soon."

"Is there any news about that?" Isa asked anxiously.

The Bey gave an angry gesture with his hand.

"Wouldn't it be better for us to go to the estate?" Susan Hanem asked.

"No one knows what's best," he answered languidly.

Events moved on until the King left the country. Isa saw

it in Alexandria. He also saw for himself the Army movements and the clamorous demonstrations. Conflicting emotions kept preying on his mind, sweeping him around in a never-ending whirlpool. The exhilaration he frequently felt was difficult to confirm, to define, or even to contemplate: though it cured the pains of his own resentment, it did not last, always collapsing against some dark cloud of other emotions. His pleasure was spoiled to a certain degree. Was this the natural reaction to the release of bitter feelings? Or was it the sort of pity that anyone might feel, standing secure over the corpse of a tyrannical rival? Perhaps when we achieve a major goal in our lives, we also lose a reason for our enthusiasm for living. Or could it be that he found it hard to acknowledge a great victory without his party taking the main credit for it?

This was the state of mind Isa was in when Abd al-Halim Pasha's visitors arrived at the latter's mansion in Zizinia.* Their feelings seemed very mixed; some of them were delighted, while others looked apprehensive and even worried.

"Glory to Him who never ceases," the Pasha said.

"Faruq's finished," Shaikh Abd as Sattar as Salhubi said in his oratorical manner, "but we need to reassure ourselves."

The ensuing wave of nervous chuckles was devoid of joy. Isa was sitting beside his friends, Samir Abd al-Baqi, Abbas Sadiq, and Ibrahim Khairat. "What about the future?" he asked.

"It will undoubtedly be better than the past!" Abd al-Halim Pasha replied, ignoring the point of the question.

"Maybe he's asking about our own future," Shaikh Abd as-Sattar as-Salhubi said to the Pasha.

"We'll have a role to play," the Pasha replied with an expressionless face, which suited an old politician. "There's no question of that."

Shaikh Abd as-Sattar trembled like a Qur'an reader steeling himself during interludes in recitation. "This movement isn't in our interests," he commented angrily. "I can smell danger thousands of miles away. On the day the treaty was annulled, we lost the King and the British, and now today we're going to lose everything."

"We're the last people who should have to worry about any danger. Or at least that's how it should be."

"We would have done exactly the same as what has happened today," Ibrahim Khairat said, "if only we'd had the strength."

"Yes, but we didn't, Sidi Umar!"* Shaikh as-Sattar retorted sarcastically.

With sudden, hammering violence, the past surged up in Isa's mind, crammed full now of glory and grief, a past, his heart told him, that was taking shape as a bubble about to burst, as a new kind of life from within revealed its outer surface bit by bit, a life charged with new and very strange notions. He could know this new way of life—he had already seen hints of it here and there—but how could it get to know him when he was still inside this bubble and it was about to burst?

His eyes rested on a picture hanging on the wall over the cold heater. It showed a black woman—thick lips and big eyes, not bad-looking. She was leering down at him with a saucy sensuality that spelled out enticement and seduction.

SEVEN

To Isa the atmosphere seemed to be weighed down with a variety of conflicting probabilities, which somehow combined to rob him of his peace of mind. He suffered through his life with his nerves on edge. The postponement of his marriage had become inevitable until such time as the earth had settled under his feet again and his father-in-law had become aware of reality again. Question marks kept springing up in front of his eyes and those of his friends like black flags on the beach when the sea is rough. They all chewed over rumors like colocynth.* Then he learned not only that his cousin Hasan had been selected for an important post but that the way was clear for him to be appointed to even more important and influential positions. As proof that Hasan belonged to this new world, this particular news stunned Isa even more than the events that had given that world birth. For a while, he did not know how to tell his mother about it, but the old lady did not understand how things really were. "Your turn will come," she said naïvely. "Don't be sad. You deserve all the best."

How nice it would be, he told himself, for a man to live far from the realm of his own consciousness. Then the purging statute was announced. He read it with a frenzied attentiveness and bitter despair: the destruction threatening the parties and leaders would destroy him as well: the roots that kept him fixed to the ground would be torn up one by one. What strange things were happening! Here was his friend Ibrahim Khairat, a lawyer and ex-member of Parliament, writing enthusiastically about the revolution in more than

one newspaper, as though he were one of the officers himself!
Attacking the parties—his own among them, of course—and
the past era as though he himself had never been a part of it.
Abbas Sadiq, calm and peaceful, a man who had not taken
any notice of the events, had found a shield to protect him
and had even continued his ambitious quest for promotion
with greater hopes than he'd had before. Only Samir Abd al-
Baqi, a thin, slender young man with a yellowish complexion
and a dreamy look in his green eyes, had suffered the same
fate as Isa and shared his own anxious fears. In him Isa found
some consolation. "What will happen to us, do you think?"
he asked.

"Dismissal is the least we can expect," Samir replied with
a pallid smile.

"What should we do?" he asked with a dry throat.

"A worthless salary. But we might find a job with a company."

"I wonder if that could be arranged for us. Could we find
the courage to start at the very beginning all over again?"

His friend shook his head. There were even a few gray
hairs among the black.

"Maybe events will prove us wrong," Isa muttered spirit-
lessly.

Complaints piled up in the office of the Purge Committee
like so much refuse. Isa gathered that most of them were
aimed at him. This did not surprise him, however, in view of
the nature of the situation. Of the people who now held senior positions in the ministry, more were his enemies than
were his friends. To those he could add the spiteful and the
jealous as well as others who would volunteer for any opportunity to inflict some damage. Some of these people defied
him openly in the ministry for no particular reason and made
sarcastic remarks about him to his face. Even a few of his
subordinates considered themselves permitted to look on him

with contempt. All this turned the ministry into a corner of hell itself.

Then he was summoned to appear before the Purge Committee. It was seated behind a green table that stretched across the room in the office of the legal adviser to the ministry. The secretariat occupied one end of the table; he was asked to sit down facing the members of the committee, who sat on the opposite side. On the wall behind them, he noticed that God's name in a frame had taken the place of the King's picture. When he looked at the faces of the people sitting in front of him, he recognized the representative of the State Council as an old colleague of his on the Students' Committee; they had both almost been killed one day during a demonstration in front of the Parliament building—and his mouth felt a little less dry. The committee only looked at him gravely, however, or glanced into their dossiers. None of them gave the slightest indication of having worked with him, even though the personnel director and the director of the general administration numbered among them. There'd been a time when he'd made several members of this committee tremble even when his party was not in power. But now a cold neutrality had taken the place of sympathy or cordiality: an icy terror pervaded the atmosphere of this big room with its high ceiling and dark walls, filled with the smell of stale cigarettes. Through the glass of the locked door, he saw a kite land on the outside balcony and then take off again at great speed, making a noise like a dirge.

The chairman stared at him for a long time through his dark blue gold-rimmed spectacles. "I hope you're completely convinced of our impartiality," he said. "We seek only justice."

"I've no doubts of that," Isa replied, a calm smile concealing his desperation.

"I want you to know that the purpose of the task with

which we have been entrusted is to serve the public interest. There's no idea of revenge or any other motive ..."

"I've no doubts about that either," Isa replied, sinking several levels further into the clutches of despair.

A gesture was made toward the secretariat and then the petitions were read out one after the other. Some of them came from civil servants, others from *umdas*.* The voice of the person who was reading them out became as monotonous as the *faqih** who intones advice to the dead at funerals. In an attempt to concentrate, Isa closed his eyes. All the accusations applied to the appointment of *umdas* on the basis of party bias and gifts, and, in the midst of so much repetition, his concentration lapsed, melting into the darkness he'd chosen by closing his eyes, which felt as if arrows were piercing them through a red fog. His efforts to regain his concentration were thwarted then by something he remembered from early childhood. It sprang up in his mind as fresh and vivid as some tender plant like youth itself: he was coming home from a game of football in the open country around Al-Way-iliyya, the rain was pouring down in torrents, and the only protection he could find was under a refuse cart. Asking himself what it meant, he opened his eyes and saw faces wavering up and down; it looked to him for an instant as though the left side of the legal adviser's mustache was connected to the right side of the State Council representative's. He was asked for his opinion. What opinion? "Rubbish! All of it!" he shouted in fury. "I would like to see one piece of proof." With this vigorous outburst, however, his energy was exhausted and he collapsed like a wilted leaf.

"The minister relied on your nominations," the chairman commented, "so you were primarily responsible."

"That was one of my duties and I carried it out in a way that satisfied my own conscience."

"Is there any other criterion—apart from party bias—to account for the appointment and dismissal of *umdas*?"

"Suppose party politics were the criterion," he replied, trying desperately to control his erratic breathing, his trembling. "Wasn't that one of the mainstays of our past life?"

"Are you satisfied with the propriety of your conduct?"

"I consider that it was quite normal."

"What about the gifts?" the chairman asked, playing with a Parker pen in his hand.

"I told you that was rubbish," Isa retorted angrily. "I'd like to see one piece of evidence."

The names of *umdas* themselves who were witnesses were read out.

"What's the point of this vulgar intrigue?" Isa yelled.

Afterward, civil servants who had worked with him for some time were called in to give testimony, then his own signatures were shown to him, on authorizations for promotion of civil servants in exceptional circumstances, orders for irrigation and farming services, and recommendations on behalf of provincial criminals connected to party hacks by patronage or kinship. As time dragged on, things began to lose their color.

"Show me a single government civil servant who deserves to stay on," he blurted out nervously, his voice too loud.

A member of the committee whom he did not know turned to him and gave him a stern lecture about a civil servant's duties toward the people. "The revolution is determined to purge the governmental machine of all kinds of corruption," he said. "I assure you that in the future no Egyptian will be deprived of his rights or gain any kind of benefit or concession for himself through belonging to any group, family, or organization."

Something deep inside Isa warned him not to argue with

this member of the committee, and so he remained silent. The investigation went on until four o'clock in the afternoon and then he left the committee room, feeling like a dried-up twig snapped off and devoured by worms. Crossing town toward Dokki, he felt as if he were floating in some sort of Atlantis. The lifeless streets, their lengths and widths, the neighborhoods they intersected, seemed remote, submerged beneath the seething clash of his own self. All he could see, hear, or think about was this unrelenting anxiety that tormented him.

"Why don't you talk to your cousin about the situation?" his old mother asked. "He's one of them!"

Her advice stung him, and he was aware that an insane look of rage flashed in his eyes.

EIGHT

The personnel director called him in to tell him that the decision had been taken to pension him off, crediting him with a two-year addition to his period of service. This was the same director who had written the memoranda connected with Isa's advancement, through promotion by exceptional promotion, all the way up to the second grade; he might still have the draft memorandum about his promotion to the first grade which had been prepared for submission to the cabinet, Isa knew, one week before the treaty had been annulled— the promotion that, in the course of events that had followed the annulment of the treaty, there had been no chance to confirm. The director himself had no party affiliation. Isa did not doubt for a moment, however, that the man loathed him: they held the same rank, after all, despite the enormous difference in their ages. He seemed moved by the situation and took advantage of the fact that there was no one else in the room to say so. "God only knows, Isa," he said, "how really sorry I am!"

Isa thanked him. He knew perfectly well the man was lying. Eight years of dealing with civil servants was quite enough to make him expert at translating their stock phrases of courtesy into what they really meant. There was his file thrown down on the desk with his name written on the cover in Persian script: ISA IBRAHIM AD-DABBAGH. In his imagination, he pictured it being thrown into the Records Office, where it would be buried forever, along with old signatures that testified to his distinction and gave promise of a happier future. He asked the director how much his pension would be.

"Twelve pounds," he was told, "but you'll also receive your full salary for a period of two years."

He left the ministry building, his eyes fixed on something inside his head, resigned to the fact that he had been destined to live through one of those lurches in history when it makes some important leap forward but forgets about the people it bears on its back, not caring whether they manage to hang on or lose their balance and fall off.

He wandered aimlessly for a while in the sunlight, oblivious of the identity of the streets he walked along, then thought of his favorite café, El Bodega, and headed in that direction. As it was noon, there was no hope of finding any of his friends there, and so he sat down and ordered a tea by himself, with his own melancholy image in the polished mirrors to keep him amused. A group of backgammon players, hovering with bated breath over the next throw of the dice, provided an appropriate example of the total indifference with which the world regarded his troubles.

He turned away from them and from the other people there who were drowning themselves in *nargila** smoke. He stared at his own dismal reflection. If this image could speak, he thought, then I would really find a person who understood me. Tell me, what have you done? Why didn't you read the future when it was only a few hours away from you, you who can confirm things that happened on this earth millions of years ago? This face, with its big head and triangular shape, praised by a poet and likened to the Nile Delta; this face which had been a contestant for front-page coverage in the newspapers, how could it possibly fall into oblivion like some dinosaur? Or like the tea you are drinking which has been pulled out of the good earth in Ceylon to get stuck eventually in the Cairo sewers? If you go up several thousand feet into space, you cannot see anything living on the earth's surface or hear a single sound; everything fuses into a cosmic insignificance. All indications point to the fact that the mighty past which is still breathing around your face will dissolve in the near future and decay. All that will remain will be a foul smell.

"My heart told me I'd find you here," a raised voice said nervously. Samir Abd al-Baqi came up and sat down beside him. He looked haggard and dispirited, almost as though he were looking at him through bars. Isa was so delighted to see him that he shook his hand fiercely in a manner that seemed to be a plea for help as well.

"My heart told me I'd find you here!" Samir repeated with more assurance.

Isa laughed loudly, so loudly that the café owner behind the table blinked. "After today," he said, "this is the only place you'll find me."

Samir gave him a mortified look with his green eyes. "It's the same with me," he said. "I left the ministry for the last time today."

They looked at each other for a long while, each of them plunged in despair. Then Isa had a feeling of mirth; it seemed strange and not really genuine, as though he had been drinking or taking drugs.

"What's to be done?" he asked.

"We've two years' grace on full salary."

"What about afterwards?"

"We may be able to find a job with a company."

"Which company will risk taking us on?" Isa asked doubtfully.

"There's a solution to every problem," Samir replied with a sigh.

Isa started on his way home. He looked at people with curiosity as though he were seeing them for the first time. They were strangers and had nothing to do with him; nor had he anything to do with them. He was an outcast in his own big city, banished without really being banished. He was amazed at the way the ground had suddenly collapsed under his feet like a puff of dust and how the pillars which had withstood fate for a quarter of a century had crumbled. When he got home, he looked at his mother's withered face and then sprang the news on her. She put her hand on the top of her head as though she were trying to stop the mounting pain. "Why are they doing that to you, my son?" she asked with a sigh.

Fortunately she did not know anything. Walking slowly around the house, he thought about how expensive it was. He couldn't possibly keep it now. Two years' salary, even added to what was left in the bank of the *umdas'* gifts, wouldn't last longer than two years. All those objects decorating the entrance, the reception room, and the library were "gifts" too. Certainly the crooks outnumbered the people who had been dismissed for crookedness. He was guilty, though, and so were his friends: what had happened to the good old days? Gifts were forbidden, after all, a mark of corruption. But this sudden loss of everything, just when he was on the very threshold of a senior position, which would have led to the minister's chair! How could you live in a world where people forgot or pretended to forget, where there were so many others who gloated over the whole thing with unfeeling malice, where hard-won honors were being stripped away and vices trundled out and exposed, unfurled like so many flags?

In the afternoon, he went to Ali Bey Sulaiman's villa. The sky was lined with clouds and a chill breeze stirred up the dust blowing like the khamsin* winds. As he climbed the broad marble steps, he thought to himself that if it were not for judicial immunity, Ali Bey Sulaiman would have been thrown into the street along with him. The Bey was outside, but Susan Hanem was in bed with a chill. Salwa appeared in a blue velvet dress. Her face gleamed out from the top of the dress like a beam of light—beautiful, but so expressionless that he could detect no reaction to recent events. His worried heart fluttered when he saw her and a spasm of love throbbed inside him like an escaped melody. He told himself she was the only thing of value he had left, and in the very next moment asked himself if she really belonged to him! "Salwa," he blurted out abruptly, anxious to put an end to any doubts, "they pensioned me off today."

Her beautiful, languid eyes blinked. "You?" she whispered in astonishment.

"Yes, me. The same thing is happening to many people these days," he said, entrusting things to fate.

"But you're not like the others!" she replied, staring at him.

Her words stabbed like a spear through the eye, and his mind reeled, his thoughts hanging suspended only by the gifts and the bank balance. "They're taking advantage of us in the name of the purge," he said.

Salwa glanced casually up at the bronze statue of a Maghrebi* horseman mounting his steed, as if asking it for an opinion. "What an insolent thing to do," she murmured.

"I'll find a better job than the one I've got at the moment," he went on, feeling encouraged.

She smiled at him as if to apologize for always seeming so listless. "Where?" she asked.

How much did she really love him? What new betrayals would the days ahead hold for him? A man's image suddenly intruded into his consciousness and under his breath he cursed the chairman of the Purge Committee. "With a company or else in some private-sector enterprise," he replied.

The tip of her tongue showed as she moistened her lips,

an action so unstudied as to suggest that for a moment she had lost interest in the impression she was making. He was aware of how disappointed she must be. "Let me draw some strength from you," he said hopefully.

Only her mouth smiled. "I wish you success," she murmured.

He put his hand over hers on the arm of the chair. "Love," he said in something close to a whisper, "can scoff at problems like these quite easily."

"Yes, yes . . ."

She might have been a little phlegmatic by nature, but she undoubtedly loved him. Overwhelmed by an urge to clasp her, he leaned forward and put an arm around her. She gave him a velvety look, surrendered her body to his arm, and a spark of sudden lust shot out from deep down in his troubled soul. He lowered his eager lips against the softness of hers and released himself to a passionate craving for consolation. But she reached up a hand to stop him, turning her face away to escape from this frenzied onslaught; they drew apart, panting, then sat back in an awful silence, during which each read the thoughts in the other's eyes, reprimand on her part and apology on his. His voice emerged broken from the confusion. "Salwa," he said, "I love you. My entire life is embodied in one thing—you."

She patted his hand sympathetically.

"You should say something," he said.

She sighed deeply and seemed to regain composure. "We must face up to life," she said, "and everything in it."

He heard the sweet melody of her voice with a profound calm. He would have liked them to leave the world and go to some unknown place forever; a place where there were no politics, no jobs, no revolutions, and no past. "Will you give me your trust and encouragement?" he asked, the first signs of cheerfulness in his voice.

"You can have what you want and more," she replied, dabbing her lips with a handkerchief.

He wanted to embrace her again, but Ali Bey Sulaiman's voice was heard outside announcing that he was about to come in.

NINE

The Bey came toward them half smiling and stayed for a short while, then called Isa away for a talk in his study, a room set far back from the street and so dark that the Bey put on the lights. Isa looked at him anxiously and read a deep concern in his eyes. He asked himself whether it had anything to do with him or was merely the result of recent events: looking up, he noticed that a picture of the Bey in his judicial uniform had taken the traditional place of the King.

"How are things?" the Bey asked.

"I'll start afresh," Isa replied, pretending to make light of things. He told the Bey about his unhappy situation, as he saw it.

The Bey thought for a while. "You won't find things easy," he said.

"I know that, but I'm not discouraged."

The Bey looked extremely serious. "To tell you the truth," he confessed, "your news didn't come to me as a surprise."

"Did the chairman of the committee tell you, sir?"

"Yes."

"Wouldn't it have been possible . . ."

"Certainly not. It's true he's a friend, but the committee's more powerful than the chairman. And everyone's afraid."

"In any case," Isa said bitterly, "what's happened has happened. Let's think about the future."

"That's the best thing you can do."

"I've spoken to Salwa about it," said Isa, taking on the unknown.

"Salwa! Did you really tell her?"

"It was only natural."

"Everything?" the Bey asked after a pause.

Isa looked at him warily. "Of course!" he replied, rather unnerved.

"What did she say?"

"Exactly what I would have suspected," he replied, inwardly considering all the possible options. "She's with me at all times, good and bad."

The Bey drummed with his fingers on the glass-covered top of the desk. "I want to be perfectly frank with you," he said. "Marriage is now quite out of the question!"

"That's true at the moment, of course!"

The Bey shook his head, as though, in addition to what he had stated so frankly, there was something else, something that he was keeping hidden.

"I'm a political victim," Isa said, trying to probe deeper.

The Bey raised his bushy eyebrows without saying a word.

"It's often been my privilege to be in this situation," Isa continued, stung to anger.

"It wasn't just politics this time," the Bey retorted.

Their eyes met and they stared at each other uneasily, while a new wave of fury came over Isa. "Explain further, please," he asked in a quavering voice.

"You know what I mean, Isa," the Bey replied, in a voice filled with exasperation and sorrow.

"Have you any doubts about me?" Isa barked, in a tone that seemed to make even the corners of this sedate room sit up and listen.

"I didn't say that."

"Then what are you driving at?"

"All the evidence looks grave," the Bey replied, frowning at Isa's tone of voice.

"It's not just grave," Isa shouted. "It's despicable—so despicable that it takes a despicable mind to digest it!"

"Your nerves are obviously—"

"My nerves are like iron, and I mean every word I'm saying."

"If you make me angry, you will truly regret it!"

His chances of having Salwa had been reduced to a hundred to one. "I don't care how things are," he yelled, "or how grave the evidence is you've mentioned. I've never been an opportunist for a single day. And the ex-King had no—"

The Bey leapt to his feet, his face black with anger, and he pointed to the door with a quivering arm, wordless. Isa left the room.

In spite of this scene, Isa decided not to give in to despair before making one final effort to defend the sole corner of consolation that had not yet been destroyed for him: the last word had to come from Salwa and no one else. Neither the strength of her character nor the depth of her love gave him great expectations, but he phoned her next day in the afternoon. "Salwa," he pleaded, "I've got to see you immediately."

Back came her answer like a slap in the face.

TEN

"There must be a solution to every problem!" Ibrahim declared as they sat in their private corner at El Bodega. Ibrahim was so small that for his feet to touch the floor he had to sit close to the edge of his chair, with the brow of his oversized head furrowed to give him a stern and serious air and thus discourage any would-be jesters from poking fun at him. The four men had piled their coats on two adjacent chairs and sat there in the crowded, noisy café with their heads close together. Ibrahim Khairat could feel relaxed when talking about problems and how to solve them, Isa told himself; the recent earthquakes had not caused any losses in his world. He was a successful lawyer and a brilliant journalist. It was the same with Abbas Sadiq, who was secure in his job even though he'd been grabbing money from more people than Isa himself. There was no envy, resentment, or anger to disturb their firm friendship, however, or their long-standing political camaraderie.

Samir Abd al-Baqi took a handful of peanuts from a heaped saucer. "That's all very well," he said. "But the days keep rolling by without our finding a real solution."

Isa looked through the window at the drizzle falling outside. "Do we start at the beginning of the road, on a typewriter?"

Abbas Sadiq began puffing at a *nargila* and blowing smoke, joining the orchestra of smokers already in the café. Smoke hung like fog around the lamps suspended from the ceiling. Isa surveyed the café, scrutinizing people's faces and their different expressions, the daydreamers looking drowsy, the people playing games with looks of fierce concentration. Why was it his fate, he asked himself in dismay, to swim against the current of history, which has been flowing for eternity? He looked out through the windowpane onto the street, inundated by rain and light, and examined with lust a woman hurrying for shelter in the dark entrance of a building. "Winter's beautiful," he said, "but Cairo isn't ready for it."

"Don't forget," Ibrahim Khairat said to Abbas Sadiq, "that our men are scattered around on the boards of directors of several companies."

Here he was talking about them and saying "our men" while at the same time writing articles attacking parties and partisanship and trying to rub out the old days altogether. Loathing reaches a very low ebb when it leads to utter disgust, but then disgust itself is an important element in loathing. The confusing exception was his own past life—and theirs—which had been marked by affection and magnanimity.

"Tell me what your feelings are," Isa asked, "when you read your articles in the newspapers?"

"I ask myself why God willed Adam to appear on the earth!" Ibrahim Khairat answered quite calmly, ignoring everyone's grins.

Abbas Sadiq raised his head from the mouthpiece of the *nargila*. He was pudgy, white-faced, his protruding eyes gleamed like a symptom of disease, and he was completely bald, with an overall appearance that would have led you to believe he was at least ten years older than he actually was. "We'll all be unhappy," he said, "till we see you both installed in two important posts with a decent company."

Trying to penetrate into the minds of these people who were clustered for no apparent reason in this café, Isa let his own mind wander through past millennia, questioning their meaning, and was at first perplexed, then alarmed. He turned again toward the window. A beggar was standing outside, giving him an imploring look. The rain had stopped. "Just imagine," Isa said to his friends, "these human beings are originally descended from fish!"

"But aren't there still millions and millions of fish crowding the oceans?"

"That's the real cause of our tragedy," he replied firmly, dismissing the beggar with a wave of his hand. "Sometimes," he continued, "it gives me great comfort to see myself as a Messiah carrying the sins of a community of sinners."

"Are you sure of the historical facts?" Abbas Sadiq asked.

He'd been sure enough, he told himself, when that telephone was slammed down.

"This would be a good time for some brandy!" said Ibrahim Khairat.

With a little water, Samir Abd al-Baqi washed down a mouthful of peanuts. "Even supposing we did do wrong," he said, "couldn't they find anything in our past records to compensate for our conduct?"

Isa closed his eyes to hear the past, its living heartbeats, the seemingly endless roar of glory, the rocketlike hiss and crack of soldiers' truncheons. There had been self-destructive enthusiasm, then sedition sapping at aspirations, with apathy creeping forward like a disease, followed by earthquakes without even the uneasy howl of a dog's warning. And the hollow-hearted search for consolation. And finally the buzz of the telephone line, the source of a void.

"We were the vanguard of a revolution," Samir Abd al-Baqi said, "and now we're the debris of one!"

"I say we should keep up with the procession," said Ibrahim Khairat, as though in a general way he was trying to justify his own position.

A sorrowful look appeared in Samir Abd al-Baqi's green eyes. "We're fated to die twice," he said.

"That's true," said Isa, endorsing his view, "and that's why we're fed on fish!"

They noticed the shoeshine man banging his box on the floor alongside them and resorted to silence till he had gone, when Samir Abd al-Baqi aroused their curiosity by laughing out loud. "I remember I once almost joined the military college!" he said.

They all laughed.

"How do you think I can feel so cheerful," quipped Ibrahim Khairat, "when things are getting darker and darker?"

Offering condolences, Isa told himself, is not the same thing as being bereaved yourself. Leaving the café at about ten in the evening, wrapping his coat around him, he looked up at the sky and saw thousands of stars; he could smell winter in the clear air after the rain. The pavement looked washed and gleamed with grayish reflection. An invigorating wind, as cold as a gibe, brushed his face in staccato gusts. He felt very strange again and kept himself calm with the thought of the two years' full salary and the remainder of the *umdas'* gifts in the bank.

In Groppi's,* he sat down alongside Abd al-Halim Shukri and Shaikh Abd as-Sattar as-Salhubi, who was in the process of whispering the latest joke. They both asked him, perfunctorily, about the latest news. He expected the Pasha to disclose the results of the efforts he'd made to find him a job.

"Are you still happy the treaty was annulled?" the Shaikh asked ironically.

He realized that the Shaikh had an obsession with the question of the annulled treaty. All the calamities that had fallen on them stemmed from it alone.

"Events are striking our colleagues down like thunderbolts," Abd al-Halim Shukri said, and then asked, "Is our turn coming?"

Isa sipped his tea and looked at the faces of people around him enjoying food and drink. Suddenly Abd al-Halim Shukri leaned toward him. "Anticipation is better than doubt," he said.

Furiously disappointed, Isa reminded himself that in the old days all these people had come to see him with some favor they wanted done. Why on earth were they snubbing him now? As he was leaving, foxy laughter burst from the mouth of a beautiful woman, as sexy as a suggestive song. In the street, the sorrows that had bent him double when the telephone was slammed down suddenly overwhelmed him again and, in spite of the cold, he almost melted away. He had loved her without once doubting that she was worthy of his love. It was true that each had accepted the other at the very beginning on the basis of other attractions which had nothing to do with love, but he had loved her quite genuinely afterwards. She had been very quick to slam the phone down in his face. Perhaps he was lucky to have suffered this blow to the heart at the same time as the blow to his political career; it could not monopolize his feelings.

His anger over all this had begun to get so out of hand that there was no room in his mind for anything of value. How can you imagine, he asked himself, that you really want to work, as you've made these other people think? Work is the very last thing you want. Who cares if these drunkards know it? Why not tell them? But before you do that, at least start looking for distractions. Let yourself enjoy a lengthy convalescence—longer than death itself. And let whatever happens happen.

ELEVEN

His cousin Hasan came to visit him. Isa told himself that no one doing well in the world ever comes to see someone who has been left behind. So why had Hasan come? At the thought of Hasan's sister anger rose up in him, but a supreme effort enabled him to be welcoming. Their relationship alone brought them together, and he wanted to hide like a criminal, but he succeeded in putting on a happy front in spite of his nervous exhaustion. Hasan's vitality, on the other hand, seemed at its peak, and his handsome, distinctive features were flushed with confidence and success. No longer the carping defeatist, he would soon, no doubt, be generously offering sympathy!

Some instinct in Isa's mother made her take an interest in Hasan's visit, and she stopped muttering her prayers so that she could hear every word being spoken. Hasan sipped his tea, smacking his lips, then asked Isa how things were. Isa answered by laughing, but said nothing. Hasan repeated his question.

"Can't you see," Isa replied, "that I'm living like a notable?"*

"It's time you got a job," Hasan said earnestly.

Isa's mother blinked and looked hopeful; she agreed with what Hasan was saying. Isa was annoyed at her hasty reaction and asked himself suspiciously what the real reason for the visit might be, vowing that he would never agree to marry Hasan's sister even if it meant dying of hunger. "I could find work if I wanted," he replied with a false air of confidence.

"Why don't you want to?" Hasan asked, with what seemed an air of brotherly concern.

"I want a long rest, something like two years or more."

"You're joking, of course!"

"No," Isa replied. "I see no need to hurry," he went on in an irate tone of voice, "especially as my engagement has been broken off."

Hasan looked at the tree standing motionless outside the window, avoiding his friend's gaze. He said nothing.

"Had you heard the news?" Isa asked anxiously.

"Yes," Hasan replied, in a voice that showed he did not like the subject. "I heard about it. During a conversation I had in passing with Ali Bey. A most regrettable situation!" The last words sounded critical.

"I taught him a lesson he won't forget!" Isa snapped.

"I gathered as much from our conversation, although the Bey didn't mention it in so many words. But let's change the subject. Maybe the best thing is to accept the choice God has made." He looked affectionately at Isa. "I've got a job for you with a respectable company," he said.

The sudden frown on Isa's face showed Hasan that something was troubling him.

"A company that produces and distributes films," Hasan continued. "I've been chosen as deputy director, but we need a qualified accounting supervisor."

"Hasan," Isa's mother exclaimed, "that's very good of you!"

Now the picture was becoming very clear, Isa told himself. I'm to be a civil servant with him as my boss, and a husband for his sister as well. If that's the case, then death take me whenever it wishes!

"I both congratulate and thank you!" he said carefully, and then smiled apologetically. "But I must decline."

Disappointment was written all over Hasan's face and

seemed to dampen momentarily its overflowing vitality. "Won't you think about it?" he asked.

"I thank you once more, but no!"

Hasan looked at him and then at his stupefied mother. "It's a very respectable job," he said.

"I'm sure it is, but I'm determined to have a long vacation."

Hasan paused for a moment. "It's not just a job," he said. "It's also an opportunity to involve yourself in the new system. Our aim in creating this new company is to serve the government's interests."

"At the moment," Isa replied firmly, "rest is more important to me than any interest."

From junior civil servant to deputy director of a company! Isa's desire to boycott work entirely grew suddenly stronger. He knew it was insane, yet he felt even more self-destructive. He stood his ground resolutely while Hasan tried other ways to persuade him. Eventually he departed without any positive result, which left Isa with a feeling of blind joy over a momentary victory.

"I don't understand anything," his mother sighed.

"Nor do I," he replied sarcastically.

"You don't like your cousin Hasan, do you?" she asked.

"He doesn't like me either!"

"But he didn't forget his family ties at the right moment!"

"He didn't do it for nothing!"

"So what?" she retorted insistently. "His sister is better than Salwa. Have you forgotten? I wish you'd think about it."

Isa looked fixedly through the tree branches at the clouds bunched up on the horizon.

"I'm really thinking of leaving Cairo," he said vaguely.

TWELVE

For months he dithered.

"I'm thinking of going to Alexandria," he told his mother one day.

More accustomed to his strange way of speaking by now, she looked much thinner and had lost her color. "But the summer's over," she replied calmly.

"I intend to stay there, not just for the summer."

Her eyelids quivered anxiously.

"I mean for a period of time," he continued.

"But why?"

"I want to live somewhere where no one knows me and I know no one."

"I'm not at all happy about your attitude," she said irritably. "A man should face up to difficulties in some other way. There's still an opening waiting for you with your cousin."

When she saw that he was determined to go, she called on his three sisters to help, and they came hurrying over to Dokki. They were all married and carried the family stamp on their faces, the triangular-shaped features and circular eyes. They all felt a real love for Isa, not just because he was a brilliant person of whom they could feel proud, but also because he was kind enough to arrange for promotions and raises for their husbands during his period of influence. They all agreed that he should not go to Alexandria and that he should accept his cousin's proposition. "What's the point of staying in a town like a stranger?"

"Isn't it enough that I'll be able to get some rest?"

"What about your future?"

"My future's a thing of the past," he retorted.

"No, it isn't. Now you have an opportunity to recover everything you've lost!"

He raised his hand in a decisive gesture that told them to stop. "There's no point in going on like this," he said calmly. "What's new and important is the fact that I've decided to move out of this house!"

His mother's face turned pale.

"There's no sense in carrying its enormous costs any longer," he said apologetically.

"Is there any connection between that and your decision to leave?"

"No," he replied with a frown. "I regard the journey to Alexandria as a necessary cure."

"Don't let your enemies gloat over your situation," his mother pleaded. "You could certainly keep your beautiful house and your way of life if you accepted the job Hasan offered you."

He closed his eyes and said nothing; he refused to carry on a futile argument.

"You're my son," his mother continued bitterly, "and I know you. You're obstinate; you always were. You've chosen pride, however much it costs you. Well, your stubbornness has only encountered love and understanding from us here. But not everyone's like your mother and your sisters!"

He shrugged. "I'll pretend I didn't hear anything," he replied scornfully.

"You should follow God's command," she said even more pleadingly. "The power is His and He can do what He wishes; the future is in His hands. You can be happy without being an under secretary or a minister."

"Where would it be best for Mother to stay till I get back?" he said, looking at his sisters.

They kept out of the discussion. Each of them suggested that their mother should stay with her.

"I shall go back to the old house in Al-Wayiliyya," the old lady said.

"You'll never live by yourself," shouted Wahiba, the daughter most devoted to her mother.

"Umm Shalabi will never leave me," her mother replied. "I hope you'll come and visit me."

Isa remembered the old house, where they all had been born, and especially the wide courtyard with its dry, sandy floor. He did not know how to express his displeasure at his mother's idea. "Wouldn't it be best for you to stay with one of my sisters?" he asked.

"No," she replied nervously. "I'm stubborn too; it'll be better for everyone if I live in the old house."

All her daughters made it clear that they would be delighted if she would stay with them, but she paid no attention. Isa's thoughts were filled with his beautiful house. He looked at the trees outside the balcony, rustling gently against a white autumn sky that seemed to inspire a sense of melancholy. "Isn't God's curse on history?" he said to himself.

"The old house isn't suitable for someone who has been used to living here," Wahiba commented.

When Isa saw his mother's eyelids quivering, he thought she was on the point of crying. "It's perfectly suitable," she replied in a wavering voice. "We were all born there."

THIRTEEN

Everything seemed to promise a deathlike repose. Grief-stricken people are apt to welcome any kind of sedative, even if it is poison. This small, furnished flat showed that civilization was not entirely devoid of a little mercy at times. There was the sea stretching away into the distance till it sank over the horizon; from the mildness of October it derived a certain wisdom and tenderness. The walls of the flat were hung with pictures of the family of the Greek woman who owned it and every time you looked outside, you could see Greek faces on the balconies, at the windows, and in the street. He was a stranger in a district filled with strangers; that was the great merit of Al-Ibrahimiyya.* If you went out, the café with its tree-lined pavement, the vegetable market with its fresh colors, and the neat shops were also full of Greek faces and now at the end of the season you could hear the language being spoken everywhere. You could really imagine that you had gone abroad; the strangeness and unfamiliarity were intoxicating. These foreigners, of whom you had often thought badly, you had now learned to love even more than your fellow countrymen. You looked for consolation in their midst since you were all strangers in a strange country.

The choice of a flat on the eighth floor was another sign of your desire to treat the idea of traveling seriously: sections of neighboring buildings stretched as far as the Corniche,* and were low enough so that over them you could see the sea in the distance, where October had bewitched it, enchanting it into daydream. You could see the bevies of quail as well, swooping in to land exhausted at the end of their long, predestined, illusorily heroic flight. Cairo was now no more than a memory clouded by sadness, loneliness, the bitter experience you needed to keep from seeing the faces of people who would make you distressed and sleepless, or the signs of triumph that would arouse your sense of loss.

He experimented with solitude and its companions—a radio, books, and dreams. Is it possible, he wondered, to forget how to speak? Moments follow each other without any regulation, he thought; you don't know the time and hardly even remember what day it is. And so you look up bewildered at the sun's tranquil diamond disk appearing behind the light clouds of autumn, life flirting with you even though you are too morose to respond. It's as though you were seeing the world—and the people in it—for the first time after waking up from a fever, an illness caused by struggle and ambition, its essential values uncovered, revealing the brilliance of creation. Up till now, the sun's course has been merely a messenger, bearing news of the submission of a memorandum, the warning of a diplomatic reception. Now that events have buried you alive, these troubles are no more than muddled dreams burning away inside your own decomposing head.

There was real loneliness in this Greek flat, and yearning in his heart. He missed the comfort of the corner in El Bodega, but his conflicting emotions connected with it seemed mean. I love Abbas Sadiq and Ibrahim Khairat, he thought, and yet at the same time I hate them! I love the part of them that was alive before the revolution, but I hate the way they've been able to live after it has taken place. Now I have an opportunity to clarify these vexing problems. Anxieties like mountains, the mind overwhelmed by rust, and the road to consolation, which is beset with folly, is paved and ready in the face of your ill-gotten gains and daydreams in which torture leads eventually to victory. A look from above at this boundless wilderness gives the soul a feeling of repose and an ability to rise above it all. O Lord, why don't You give us a gleam of inspiration about the meaning of this grueling journey stained with blood? Why doesn't the sea say something when it has seen the struggle going on since time immemorial? Why does this mother earth eat up its sons when evening comes? How is it that rocks, insects, and the condemned man in the mountain* have a role in the drama while I have none?

One morning he went to the Paradise Casino in Gleem* in response to a letter from Samir Abd al-Baqi. He hadn't seen Samir since coming to Alexandria in the middle of September and hadn't visited the Paradise Casino since the summer of 1951. There was no one on the beach and the casino itself was almost empty, as was usual during the final days of October. In his period of influence, Isa had gone to the Paradise with an arrogant air, and people would look at him with interest as he made his way between pashas—friends and enemies—to the table reserved for him in that ephemeral world. How could people forget the reception at the Paradise two years ago? The fabulous sound, the all-embracing magnificence of it all and the ringing shouts, and then his own arrival with an entourage to drink, have fun, and while away the evening. All he had seen on the horizon then were hopes that had held the promise of sure success.

He sat in his old place to the right of the inside entrance, among the empty seats. Some old pashas, who were hanging on till the last moment of the summer season, were sitting at scattered tables; two women sat by themselves, one old, the other middle-aged. A dreadful silence hung over the whole place. Isa stole a look at the old woman and told himself that Salwa would meet the same fate one day, going the way of all prestige and power, of all expectation. He took pleasure in looking at the expanse of sea, calm and pure blue, and at the clouds, which looked as though they might be swollen with white rose water.

Samir Abd al-Baqi arrived on time and they embraced warmly. Samir looked even thinner than when he'd seen him last, but he was in better health and his eyes looked clearer. "My wife and I are here visiting her mother," he said. "We're going back tomorrow."

Isa asked about the corner in El Bodega and Samir replied that there was nothing new. "I've sold my share in an old house," he said, "and gone into partnership with an uncle who sells furniture. In fact, I'm his accounts manager and a junior partner."

Isa congratulated him and told him that he himself had no desire to work at the moment.

"Just look how empty Alexandria is!" Samir said, gazing around.

"The whole world's empty," Isa replied. "What's that you're holding?"

Samir handed him a book and he read the title *Ar-Risalat al-Qushairiyya** on the cover. Isa looked inquiringly at him.

"Haven't you heard of mysticism?" Samir asked.

Isa laughed abruptly. "I never knew you were interested in it," he said.

"I wasn't, but then I heard Ahmad Pasha Zahran discussing it. He's given me some books on the subject at various times and recently I've found myself looking into them."

"Are you serious about it," Isa asked with some vestiges of laughter still visible on his face, "or is it just a question of amusement?"

Samir emptied a bottle of Coca-Cola into his glass. "It's more than just amusement," he replied. "It's a real source of relaxation." He drank half the glass and then continued. "The fact that you only look to it under the constraint of specific circumstances doesn't negate its qualities. We may only go to Aswan in winter to cure an illness, but that in itself doesn't discredit the benefits which Aswan can offer whether we're sick or healthy."

"But there's obviously a difference," Isa said mockingly, "between turning to mysticism during a political crisis and doing so quite spontaneously when things are going well."

Samir smiled patiently, his green eyes glinting even more brightly than the candescent clouds. "Yes, there's a difference," he said, "but the lesson's in the consequences. Sometimes a disaster will hit us in such a way as to lead us unawares along the right path!"

"Suppose, for example, that the world ..." Isa stopped speaking suddenly, as though he'd stumbled on silence, caught up in an exchange of glances with the middle-aged woman who was sitting next to the old one. Then he turned back to his friend, thinking that if things had gone as he'd wanted, Salwa would have been his wife now for at least a year. If only ...! "What is the mystical view of the particle 'if only'?" he asked.

Samir did not understand his point, so Isa gave the answer himself. "'If only' is the particle of anguish which has stupidly hankered after some illusory ability to change history."

"From the mystical point of view," Samir replied simply, "it represents a denial of God's manifest will in history. What it does is to imbue things with futility and irrationality."

Salwa has not budged from your heart, Isa thought to himself, even though you despise her character. The mind may formulate specifications for the ideal woman however it likes, but love is an essentially irrational proceeding—like death, fate, and chance. Salwa's behavior was typical of this world. You'll still need girls, though; they're wonderful tranquilizers for anxieties. Probably better than mysticism, he thought, remembering the question he'd broken off. "Suppose," he said, "the world promised us we'd be appointed to the ministry again! What would you do with mysticism?"

Samir laughed so hard that his teeth flashed. "It isn't difficult to do both at once," he replied. "That's what Ahmad Pasha Zahran used to do. Now you see me combining mysticism with commerce. It doesn't stifle your energies, but gets rid of flaws."

"It's better than suicide, at any rate," said Isa sadly.

The sun shone for a few seconds, then disappeared again. Samir asked him what he intended to do.

"Are we really finished?" Isa asked him in turn.

"Most probably," Samir replied, shaking his head in despair. "Things aren't as they were in previous revolutions."

Isa said nothing for a while, as though he were listening to the all-pervading silence. "We're just like the Alexandria beach in autumn," he said.

"That's why I'm saying you should get a job."

"We won't be working, whatever job we take," Isa replied, "because we've no role to play. That's why we feel excised and rejected like a removed appendix." He gave a smile, then continued. "I must confess that I have my own mystical beliefs. They keep me busy when I'm alone."

Samir looked concerned.

"I'm thinking of taking up crime," Isa said blandly.

Samir let out a long laugh. "That's a novel form of mysticism!" he said, still chuckling.

"But you don't kill your own body with it. Just other people's."

"I suppose you'll choose some kind of sex crime."

They both laughed.

"Thank God, there's still a world that can laugh," Samir said.

"We'll laugh a lot more every time we take a look at

what's going on. It'll all be worked out for us. But we won't be participating in it. We'll be like eunuchs."

A gentle breeze blew. The pashas looked as though they were asleep. For no particular reason, Isa remembered the first speech he'd made in Parliament, when he was still a student at the university. "Our very history is threatened with extinction," he said sadly.

"History is very long-suffering. It'll defend itself when all the other combatants have disappeared."

The Greek proprietor walked over to them, smiled at Isa, and asked him how he was and how things were going. Isa recognized the political import of his question immediately. "Just as you see," he replied with a smile.

When he returned to his tall building near the tram stop, he was feeling depressed at saying farewell to Samir. As he walked through the high, dark entrance, he cursed Salwa, and as he entered the elevator, he told himself how much he needed a "tranquilizer."

FOURTEEN

He stood alone with his glass in the dimly lit corridor connecting the candy counter outside and the ballroom inside at the Petit Trianon. A big band was playing dance tunes, and couples clung to each other as they danced with light and elegant movements; in that way they could shrug off the discomforts of the sunlight. All these beautiful women belonged to houses now, not to the streets, as had been the case before and during the war. He'd begun to appreciate what was happening during his adolescence and early manhood. They'd made a lot of money during the war years and wouldn't stoop now to displaying themselves on the cheap any longer. They've disappeared from the square, leaving it vacant, Isa told himself, for people who wanted the job of making a quick profit from political outcasts! One tune made him sway and he longed to dance—something he did fairly well—but where was the beautiful partner? He took a drink of cognac, which he liked in moderation. He felt sheltered and that made him more relaxed. His little cache of money from the *umdas* would provide him with funds to indulge in some delightful escapades, he told himself. If it weren't for our morbid feelings about the future, nothing would ever bother us!

He did not enjoy his shelter alone for long. A voice caught him by surprise. "What do you think of the world?" it asked.

The shock made him shudder. He looked along the bending corridor but could not see anyone. The voice belonged to an old drunk, obviously spouting his quota of drivel. But where was he? The voice spoke again. "Do you want to know where I am?" it asked with a laugh. "Fine! I'm behind the tree."

At the bottom of the bend in the corridor that led to the candy counter was a half-grown tree—natural or artificial—in a huge pot; everything beyond the tree was total darkness, the candy counter having closed at eight in the evening. Isa deduced that the man had been sitting in the corridor and that for some reason he'd decided to move his seat into the dark to play his stupid game. He cursed the man under his breath and ignored him, but the latter began asking questions again without coming out into the dim light. "Have you ever tried drinking in the dark?" he inquired.

Isa said nothing, hoping he'd shut up.

"Drinking in the dark allows you to concentrate," the man went on. "That's why I'm thinking about the state of the world. Is it really going to ruin?"

Isa watched the dancing, half attentive, and took pleasure in the faces, breasts, and rosy complexions.

The drunk would not let go. "The question's really important to me," he said. "If it's moving to destruction, then I'll drink cognac. If there's any hope, I'd prefer whiskey. And therefore if I find myself in both situations, I'll destroy myself, because I'll be struck by three momentous diseases at once—low blood pressure, cirrhosis, and hemorrhoids!"

Isa smiled in spite of himself. It was nice to be drunk, at any rate. The trials that have descended upon us are enough to break our hearts, he thought; enough to kill us. It's as if all the debris from the collapsed old world were piling on top of your head. And the worst thing of all is the knowledge that, even though you loathe the new era, you still cannot reject it in your mind. Neither you nor your cache of *umda*s' money!

"Destruction's nothing new in the world. If it's written on your forehead, then it's better for it to be quick."

"Why do you want it, provided it's quick?" Isa asked the man almost without realizing it.

"As the proverb goes," the man replied with a boisterous laugh, "the best charity comes quickest!"

Isa pitied the victims of history with a sigh in his heart, drained his glass, and left. He walked along Saad Zaghlul Street, his favorite street in Alexandria, particularly after the revolution; his own private street, in a way, and he liked walking along it, if only once a day in each direction, so that he could be alone with his flooding memories.

It was getting close to midnight and the air had become refreshingly cool. The whole area looked deserted. He glanced at the back of the statue gazing out to sea and tossed his head back like the pasha whom he had loved to imitate in times past.

He took the tram to Al-Ibrahimiyya and then went to the Corniche for a gentle walk along the seawall to calm his nerves. The salty air rose up around his head, which was reeling from the alcohol he had drunk. The stars were shining in the wide gaps between the clouds, and the sea was calm, like someone asleep in the dark. In the distance, the rows of lights attached to the fishing boats stretched out in a line. There was no one to be seen on the road. The sense of total abandonment came back again and he sat down on a stone bench to savor this feeling of silence and sympathy. He would not go back to his empty home till drowsiness persuaded him: since coming to Alexandria, he'd been living his own life, not following anyone's orders or conforming with any customs, satisfying his own whims in absolute freedom, going to sleep when he could not stay awake any longer, waking up when he got tired of sleeping, eating when he was hungry, and going out when he was bored. He'd never enjoyed freedom like this before.

Something to his left attracted his attention, as though

some hidden temptation were trying to contact one or more of his senses—a figure coming toward him from a distance. When it came closer under the streetlight and the features became clear, he saw that it was a girl. The cheap cotton flannel dress, the defiant look untinged by reserve or haughtiness, and the very fact that she was walking alone at night, all these things showed that she was a Corniche girl. He examined her as she walked past him through the narrow space between his bench and the seawall. He could see she was young and had quite nice features, but her appearance was very common, and she had an air of ready response to some gesture that would take her in, like a stray dog looking for any passerby to follow. She walked past till she reached the next bench and sat down on it, eyes fixed in his direction. What a bunch of scavengers these whores are, Isa thought. But what else is there once the summer season is over and Alexandria folds up totally, looking as though its doors were locked in the face of strangers? Deep down inside he felt disgusted. But his pulse was throbbing insanely with desire. The director of the minister's office with designs on the minister's chair was dead and buried. That much was quite clear. All that was left of him at the moment was a drunkard alone in the dark whose desires were crawling all over like nocturnal insects. It was as though an irresistible impulse to wallow in the dust were blowing through his brain.

He signaled to her with as flirtatious a gesture as he could muster, and then repeated it. She got up and moved toward him till she stood at arm's length. He gestured to her to sit down, and she did so with a laugh as soft as the whisper of the waves that lapped below, at the foot of the seawall. He looked at her face and was shocked by its youth. "How old are you?" he asked.

She laughed without answering. He repeated the question anxiously.

"Guess!" she said.

"Maybe you're fifteen," he said.

"No," she replied proudly. "I'm not a minor, in any case, so relax."

A pale matt complexion, round face, full cheeks, small, full body, and short hair like a boy. She kept playing with her nails; the varnish on them had flaked away.

"Where did you come from at this hour of the night?"

"From the café," she replied, pointing back down the road behind her to a lighted door wrapped in darkness and silence.

"I didn't notice it as I was walking," he said.

"People heading there usually see it." She laughed. "Cigarette?"

They both lit cigarettes. He couldn't think of anything to say. "Let's go," he whispered.

They walked side by side along one of the roads leading off the Corniche. She took his arm and he winced, scowling, in the darkness, remembering Salwa. If they're sincere, he told himself, they should let free elections decide!

FIFTEEN

He woke up about noon and looked with curiosity at the naked girl sleeping next to him. Recollections of the previous night came back and he told himself that as long as oblivion and habit still existed, everything remained possible. As she lay there, almost completely uncovered, he examined her, coldly and calmly, contemptuous of everything. Her full lips were parted, revealing a neat set of teeth, but after a night's sleep her hair looked as it really was, dry, coarse, and unkempt. There was an odd physical inconsistency about her; her eyelashes were long and voluptuous, but her breasts looked chapped and flaky, like a pair of toads.

He got out of bed and went to the bathroom. When he came back, he found her sitting up in bed yawning. She lifted two beautiful, heavy eyes in his direction. He decided to get rid of her as soon as possible. "I've an appointment," he said. "I've got to go."

She looked at him, hesitated, and then left the room. He opened the balcony door and a strong breeze blew in. It felt quite pleasant, full of the smell of the sea and the warmth of the sun, which was shining in the middle of the sky. As he dressed, he looked out to sea. There was an impetuous motion to it today; the whole surface was flecked with foam and the waves looked like mouths laughing. She was a long time in the bathroom, he thought, until he went into the lounge to turn on the radio and found her there, cleaning and putting things straight with great industriousness. "Thank you," he said, "but leave that for the *bawwab*.* It's time for me to go."

"Go ahead," she replied, without stopping what she was doing.

"But when are you going to get dressed?"

She sat on a big chair in the lounge and smiled.

"You may be able to dawdle," he said, "but I've got an appointment."

"Do you live alone?" she asked quietly.

"Yes . . . but come on!!"

She started combing her hair. "I told myself you might need someone as a companion and servant," she said, showing a genuine shyness for the first time.

"Thank you," he replied in astonishment, "but I don't need anything like that. Haven't you got a home?"

"No."

"Where are you living?"

"Sometimes with the woman who owns the café," she replied shamefully, "and other times I spend the night in the café! We don't find any work in the winter, and last summer was just like winter, in any case!"

"Whatever your problem is," he snapped, "you'll find the solution outside."

She stood up. "I didn't save anything for this winter," she said quietly, "and you need someone to serve you."

Her insistence only made him more obdurate. "Why don't you go to Cairo for the winter?" he said.

She looked at him in amazement, as though the idea would never have occurred to her. "But I'm from here," she answered simply.

"Haven't you got any family?"

"Of course, but I can't go back to them!"

"Aren't you afraid one of them might see you?"

"They're in Tanta.* That's where I come from."

"If you don't mind," he said, annoyed at having let the conversation go this far, "I'm in a hurry."

As she went into the other room to put her clothes on, he remarked to himself that they were very much alike—both disgraced outcasts. When the girl came back she seemed to have despaired of arousing his sympathy and tried being playful. "Is that your family?" she asked coyly, looking at the picture of the Greek family on the wall.

He laughed in spite of himself. "What a devil you are!"

Her laugh was unexpectedly merry. Then, more seriously, she asked him, "Are you from Alexandria?"

"No."

"Then you're here as a civil servant?"

"Almost."

"Almost?"

"You're like a district attorney!" he barked. "Come on!"

She asked to be paid and he gave it to her—much less than he'd expected. He felt sorry for her for the first time since he had woken up. They left the flat together and separated at the entrance to the building. He headed straight for a restaurant to satisfy his hunger, then killed the hours between three and six at the first cinema he came to. Afterwards, he sat in the Grand Trianon drinking coffee and reading the evening paper. Around nine o'clock he went to his dark seat in the Petit Trianon corridor and listened to the music, amusing himself by watching the dancers and swilling cognac. At one point he wished that the man who'd been behind the tree the night before would raise his voice again and pour abuses on the world.

"I'm a student of Sufism* as well," he said aloud, as though he were talking to Samir Abd al-Baqi. "You're not the only one." He smiled regretfully to himself. Don't think about the future, he told himself. That's right. You're still only at the honeymoon stage. What you need is a long unbroken vacation. Don't be upset by your own insignificance. It's a historical phenomenon.

He left the place a little before midnight. As he approached the entrance to his building, he was surprised to see the girl sitting in the Greek café on the chair nearest the doorway, her face smiling in welcome. She sprang up and ran to meet him in front of the entrance. He stopped in bewilderment.

"You weren't late for your appointment?" she said.

She went in first. He hesitated a moment and then followed her. "What are you doing?" he asked.

"I was waiting for you," she replied, taking him by the arm. "If he comes back alone, I told myself, I'll be in luck."

He was pleased by her flattery, even though he was painfully aware of the situation. "What's your name?" he asked her in the elevator.

"Riri," she replied.

"That's obviously a genuine Tanta name!" he retorted with a laugh.

"It's the one I use in Alexandria."

There was a short pause.

"My heart tells me," she continued, "that you'll offer me your hospitality."

SIXTEEN

He allowed her to stay in the flat as she wished. He made it clear to her from the very beginning that he was a free man, and that she had to keep within her bounds even if he brought a woman home every night; to all of which she agreed without question. Afterwards he could not deny that she gave the flat a friendly feeling and cleanliness that had been absent before and introduced a breath of warm air into its cold atmosphere. When she wore the new clothes he bought for her, she looked really presentable, and she always took particular care of her appearance. She played her role adroitly, something above that of a servant and yet below that of mistress of the house. She avoided getting on his nerves in any way whatsoever. She shared his food, cigarettes, and drink, but did not ask for a penny apart from that. He gave her no encouragement to get emotionally involved with him or use endearing words. "I'm a man who distrusts everything," he told her. "That's the way I am, so make sure you don't lead me to suspect you're lying."

When winter took over, the weather seemed to be as unsettled as the invisible world itself. He was forced to spend long nights in the flat with her. They would listen to the radio or else he would spend a few hours by himself reading or give his exhausted feelings some relief by listening to her silly chatter. The worst thing that would happen while he was living with her was that sometimes she would suddenly strike him as a symbol of the utter humiliation into which he had sunk. When that happened, he would keep out of her way and start insulting her at the first opportunity. Her full, round face would show a frown. He would be aware of the effort she was making to keep her temper under control and suppress a desire to give vent to her aggressive instincts, instincts that she had acquired through her life on the streets. All this involved an inner struggle, traces of which were clearly visible on her cheeks and lips and in her expression and the way her features altered. Even though she was illiterate, she was well educated in the cinema and radio. She could remember the names and pictures of the various stars as well as the films, songs, and programs, and she could never have enough of talking about them. "Don't you think," she asked him, "that I'm good enough for the cinema?"

He told her that he had no experience in that field. He was amazed at mankind's power of self-deception, more powerful than the atom itself. She told him stories about the stars, and he had no idea of where she got them from; this was all to convince him that she was worthy of the bright lights and that it was a question of luck—no more and no less!

"You should be looking for a producer's or director's flat," he told her with a laugh, "so that you can share it with him!"

Since the nights were so long and he refused to go to bed before dawn, she taught him various kinds of card games. She gambled with him a great deal and won some money from him, but this was the only money from him that she ever put in her pocket.

Once it occurred to him to ask her what she knew about politics, which had swallowed him as a hero and then spat him out as a corpse. So he asked her about some names and events, but she shrugged her shoulders and did not bother to answer. He was amazed that there could be a human being in existence who did not care about the world of politics. "What do you know about the constitution?" he asked mockingly.

Her eyes showed no signs of understanding.

"What are your views on independence?" he continued.

Her look did not change.

"I mean the departure of the English," he said by way of explanation.

"Oh!" she shouted. "Let them go if you want them to. But I've heard a lot about how good things were in their day. My mistress, the café proprietress, opened her café on their money!"

For her, he thought, real independence meant being rid of the need for me and others like me.

She opened her heart to him and told him about her past with an unusual frankness. "I have a mother, aunt, and sisters," she said. "The only male relative I have left is an uncle in his nineties. So I don't expect to be killed for honor's sake." She had been a devil since she was young. Her father had died when she was ten, and her mother had been unable to control or discipline her. She could not keep her daughter away from the boys and no amount of scolding or beating was of any use. "I loved a boy before I had even reached maturity and became proverbial in the village for that reason ..." Then the inevitable thing had happened. "My mother hit me, then slapped her own cheeks until she fell to the ground as if she were dead." She had run away with the boy to Alexandria where he was going to finish his education. He got rid of her after a few months and she had found herself alone. It was then that she had begun this life.

"You're a small girl," he said with a smile, "but a big devil ..."

"An old *khwaaga** in Al-Azarita* loved me," she said proudly, "and took me on, to stay as his servant. He had an old, bedridden wife."

"But you weren't as good at making good use of opportunities as your mistress, the café proprietress."

"I seek nothing but shelter," she replied simply.

He laughed loudly and told himself that it might be useful if we could find something to convince us that we are not the most miserable of all God's creatures. "What do you expect from the future?" he asked.

She raised her eyebrows for a few moments. "Our Lord is great," she mumbled.

"You sound religious!"

She smiled at the sarcastic tone in his voice and took refuge in silence.

"But you admit yourself that you're a devil, don't you?"

She laughed heartily. "The time for sleep came along," she said, "and that's better than wearing your head out for nothing."

He became increasingly convinced of similarities that joined him and this girl together. He conceded that she was absolutely necessary and indispensable to him in his loneliness, especially when things were really bad. The ax had fallen on the leaders and the hearings were over. He felt ill at ease, like a drug distributor when he hears all of a sudden that the big operators have been arrested. He denied the world and refused to acknowledge it any longer. He was not astonished anymore by the blustery days when the harbor was closed and the angry waves in the raging sea flew up in the air and battered the Corniche. The clouds were as dark as parts of night itself and the lightning flashed incredibly like rockets. The rain came down in torrents like little creatures running away from the wrath of the heavens. It seemed blind stupidity to stay in Alexandria, and he longed to be back in Cairo and the warm corner at El Bodega.

"I wonder where you are!" she said to him. "You're not with me and you're not anywhere in the world either!"

He came back down to earth again. His expression looked tired from all this wandering around in oblivion. He gave a weak smile but said nothing.

"You've been like this for days," she said.

"Yes, I have," he replied angrily. "All you listen to on the radio is the songs!"

"Are you a notable?" she asked, in an embarrassed tone.

"Or unemployed!" he said with a dry laugh.

"You? Oh no! But you certainly are a mystery."

"They unravel mysteries."

"Tell me, how long are you going to stay like this?"

"Let me ask you the same question."

"My life isn't in my hands."

"Nor mine." He continued with a smile. "When spring comes, we'll each be on our own way."

"I won't go," she said with an unexpected intensity, "until you have me thrown out."

Blasted emotions! Sincere or false, God damn them all! Her affection for him inspired exactly the opposite reaction in him—he became almost angry. He concentrated on the song that was being broadcast. Then a program on economics was announced: a group of economists were going to hold a discussion. When, listed among the participants, he heard the name Hasan ad-Dabbagh, he rushed over to the radio and turned it off. She asked him why he was annoyed.

"I said you only listen to the songs!" he replied angrily.

On the clear winter days, he wandered around the different places in Alexandria that he loved. He did not take her with him even once, but neither did he prevent her from exercising complete freedom to move around as she wished. In her eyes he could read a desire to go out with him, even if only for a short walk on the Corniche, but he hated the very idea.

"Don't you think," she said, "that you're treating me as though I were . . ."

"Stop looking for trouble," he interrupted firmly.

Her face flushed with obvious emotion. When he noticed

it, he felt sorry for her and fondled her short hair. "Stop looking for trouble," he repeated tenderly.

She no longer expressed her feelings in words, but rather in the effort she made to serve him and tend to his comforts. He received these gestures with a gratitude mixed with distrust. Winter would soon be over, he told himself, and then he would be rid of this attachment that had infiltrated his flat. Even from his bitter experience with Salwa, there was only a surface wound left, and that may have been pride rather than love. He realized that the void which politics had left in his heart would have to be filled by some amorous escapades for a while and that might prove troublesome.

As the days passed, he was amazed to see the girl's health getting noticeably worse. She looked terrible: pale, weak, and exhausted. How could this happen when she was getting food and comfort which she had never even dreamed of? He thought she might have a cold, but none of the symptoms of a cold was apparent. The ailment stayed with her to a degree that both worried him and kept him occupied. "What's the matter with you?" he asked her. "Have you ever had anything like this before?"

She replied that she had not and kept moving away when he followed her, until suddenly she had to give up and lie down on the bed. He stood there looking at her, alarmed and angry. "I'll have to call a doctor," he said.

She gestured to him not to do that. "No," she said. "It's just that I'm exhausted by the humidity."

Tears were pouring down her face and she looked like an inexperienced child. Suddenly he felt fear gripping him for some unknown reason. "No doubt you've something to say," he said.

She shut her eyes in despair and pointed to her stomach without saying anything. His heart gave a violent thump, something it had done only during the terrible events that had finished him off. His fear turned to pure anger. Now it was quite clear what the sly little minx was after! "You poisonous little snake!" he yelled at her. "Is this how you pay me back for giving you a home?"

"I didn't realize it until some time had passed," she wailed.

"You little devil, are you pretending to be that naïve?"

"No, never," she replied, "but it happened in spite of all the precautions I took."

"You liar! Even if I believed you, why didn't you tell me?"

"I was afraid! I was so afraid, I couldn't!"

"Even devils are afraid of people like you!" he yelled. "What are you waiting for then? When are you going to do something about it?"

"I can still remember a friend of mine," she pleaded, sobbing as she did so, "who died while doing that . . ."

"So?" His voice was blocked because he was so angry. "Well then," he yelled, "reveal your cunning plan! Now, just listen to me." Then, warning her with his index finger, he said, "Don't let me see your face from now on, ever again!"

"You haven't wasted the opportunity to get rid of me now it's come," she pleaded, "but at least be kinder than that."

"From now on," he yelled like a demon, "I understand you! From now on! Never again."

SEVENTEEN

Loneliness began to weigh heavily on him. He could no longer bear returning to the flat before late at night. However, his fear of the girl was even greater than all the tortures he was going through. He started wondering whether she was going to create a public scandal. Would he soon be standing in disgrace in front of the public prosecutor? How the newspapers would relish the thought of exposing him! What a wonderful opportunity it would be to expose the others as well, and his entire era! These anxious thoughts preyed on his mind like mosquitoes in a swamp.

However, days went by without any of his fears being realized; nor did a bill for an abortion come from the girl. He knew he should return to Cairo, but for some incomprehensible reason he was determined to stay in Alexandria. Every time he felt safe as far as the girl was concerned, he clung still closer to his own sufferings. The storms no longer disturbed him so much as fascinated him, and loneliness worked its cryptic and deadly magic on him. The atmosphere of living among foreigners, with its own strange aroma, gave him dreams of emigrating forever to the mountaintops painted with green fields; there he could spend the rest of his life far away from anxieties.

He was very fond of Ramla Square;* it was a permanent stage for elegantly dressed women with golden tresses wrapped up in their raincoats. Every time a tram came, flocks of beautiful women would emerge; it made Isa feel more relaxed and almost drunk as their legs seemed to play all kinds of tunes to him. When a policeman noticed him staring at a gorgeous girl and getting ready to follow her, their eyes met, and the policeman smiled. Isa suddenly came to himself as he remembered the awe that he had inspired in all ranks of policemen in the old days. He took a seat behind the window in 'Ala Kaifak* which looked out onto the square, where streams of humanity kept crashing into each other. From his vantage point, he could live among them as he liked without getting tired. In his past life, weighed down by ambition, he had had no chance to sit down like this, even though all he was really doing now was sitting there like some discarded foam left behind on the beach by a wave for the municipal workers to come by and scoop up. Where were the key power figures who had been forced to go into hiding? When would people stop crying about them? These days, the game could only be undertaken on impulse, without relish or real human contact. When time did allow some human relationships to be formed, the hurricane would rage and everyone standing up would be blown away.

The sky was getting darker now. Some unknown force was swallowing up all the daylight; clouds were gathering, and human beings could be seen scurrying away like ghosts. Alexandria! Your winter is as fickle as a woman! The wind blew hard, like bad news. People wrapped their coats around them. Newspaper vendors closed up their stands; it became the ultimate in blessings to take refuge behind the window of 'Ala Kaifak and sip hot tea. The thunder rumbled, and people started. Down came the rain, but with a certain grace to it; the space between the sky and the earth seemed to be fixed to electric wires. The square was empty, and the people huddled together gave him a warm feeling; he felt relaxed and at ease.

He heard a slight cough and turned to his left. There was Riri, sitting at a table only one away from his! He quickly looked toward the square, but, in his churning thoughts, she was the only thing he could see, wearing that old orange coat of hers. She had only turned around for a moment, but her smiling eyes were full of tragedy. Was she following him on purpose, or had she simply wandered aimlessly across his path? Would it all end peaceably, or burst into a public scandal? Had she got rid of the thing, or was she still determined to keep it?

He decided to leave, but when he looked outside he saw that the storm was still raging, and resigned himself to remaining a prisoner inside the café. He resolved to leave Alexandria at the first opportunity, the next day if he could. Then he put on a careless air and rested his cheek on his fist as though he were pondering dreamily. Suddenly, he thought that her presence there might be part of a plan she had arranged with the police so as to arrest him, that now his name would be added to those of all the outstanding members of his generation who were being thrown outside the walls one after another. That might lead to something even worse too, for they would undoubtedly examine his bank account, and then they might start asking him where the money had come from. But before he realized it, the girl was sitting down at his table. "I thought I'd invite myself over," she said, "since he doesn't want to do it himself!"

He stared at her coldly so as to hide his alarm, and said nothing.

"Don't be afraid," she said. "We can sit together for a while, as old friends should."

This was the first step in the trap, he told himself; maybe the other people involved were watching too. He decided to defend himself to the death. "What are you talking about?" he said in a voice loud enough for the people who were sitting nearby to hear. "I don't understand a thing!"

His feigned ignorance surprised her, and the jovial look went out of her eyes. "Is that all you can say?" she muttered.

He stretched out his left hand in a display of bewilderment. "Well, now," she said in amazement, "so you don't recognize me?"

"I'm sorry. Maybe you've mistaken me for someone else."

Her disappointment made her look sad. Then she closed her lips in anger, and her whole expression changed. She looked so threatening that he expected something terrible to happen in front of all the people sitting there. However, she simply got up.

"I suppose you're going to say God creates forty people who all look exactly alike, aren't you?" she said in a sarcastic and defiant tone.

He was so worked up that he felt giddy. He never thought it would end that way. Every time he remembered her changing expression, he shuddered, and felt sure that, under a happy girl's skin, a tigress was always lurking. He stayed in this daze for a long time; he had no idea how long. Eventually he noticed that the rain had stopped and a gap was opening up on the horizon. A ray of sunshine was bursting through, even though it looked thoroughly washed. He got up without delay, put his coat on, and left without looking in her direction.

It was after midnight when he got back to his building. He found a telegram waiting for him from the family to say that his mother had died.

EIGHTEEN

The funeral would be held at Al-Qubbat al-Fidawiyya on the following afternoon. Isa got there early to welcome the mourners, and his arrival coincided with that of Hasan, his cousin, in his Mercedes. Naturally the car was no surprise to Isa, but the sight of it irritated him. He was amazed at the sudden and obvious improvement in his cousin's health; an air of superiority gave him an upright bearing, and his eyes had a look of authority in them. They shook hands and stood there waiting in the shade of a tree. Hasan started looking him over. "You don't look as healthy as I would have expected!" he said.

"Perhaps the weather doesn't agree with me," Isa replied, reviewing his sorrows in a single fleeting moment.

"That was a meaningless trip to Alexandria," the young man said in a decisive and official tone of voice, "but then, you're a stubborn man."

Hasan was still hanging on to his old dream, Isa thought, of marrying him off to his sister. Then Isa's friends, Samir Abd al-Baqi, Ibrahim Khairat, and Abbas Sadiq, arrived with various former senators and representatives. Countless groups of people came to offer their condolences to Hasan, and the tent was crowded with them all, even though it was huge. There was an anxious moment when Ali Sulaiman got out of his car. Hasan welcomed him, and Isa saw no way out of greeting him too. They shook hands with each other and Isa accepted his condolences, but neither of them looked at the other once. The traditional stages in the ceremony followed, one after the other. Isa lost his composure only at the burial itself, when his eyes filled with tears in spite of the effort he made to control his emotions. He had supervised the entire proceedings himself. Unable to resist the eternal temptation, he looked at the grave pit for a long time. He wanted to be left alone to say some important things to her. He suddenly remembered the last time he had said goodbye to her in the old house. She had kissed him on the forehead. "Do whatever you want," she had said. "May the good Lord protect you wherever you are. I'll hold back my tears so that you can leave in peace!"

He could hardly remember the expression on her face because he had not been looking at her closely; but her hands had felt cold, lean, and trembling.

When the recitation started, he moved to one side, and more than once exchanged glances with his friends. He asked himself why they looked sadder than they needed to be. This, then, is the ultimate destination for everyone, he thought with a comforting enthusiasm and a certain amount of malice, for poor people and tyrants alike; yes, and tyrants too!

The condolences in the house that night were restricted to members of the family and his three friends. Ali Sulaiman did not come, and Isa avoided going to the harem so as not to see his uncle's family. Nevertheless, he wondered whether Susan Hanem and Salwa had come. The scene in the room where Samir, Abbas, Ibrahim, and Hasan were sitting with him was almost comical. None of his friends dared to express his political views in front of Hasan, and since the discussion of politics could not be avoided in any gathering, they saw no solution except to be hypocritical. So they started praising the startling historic actions of the revolution, the abolition of the monarchy, the end of feudalism, and the evacuation— especially the evacuation, that age-old dream. Isa contributed only a little to the conversation; he was exhausted and felt empty and sad. He concealed his sarcastic thoughts about the situation by pretending to listen to the Qur'an reciter, who was sitting in the lounge on the third floor. Hasan had become a key figure, he told himself, someone to really reckon with! Wasn't that laughable? He surrendered to the incredible notion that his mother had not really died, that she was still alive in some way, or that her spirit had not yet left the house. Then he recalled in amazement the old dream of the evacuation and how he had listened to the news of its announcement with a feeling of languid satisfaction mixed with anger merely because it was not his party that had brought it about. He could not help saying, "The fact is that the evacuation is really a fruit of the past!"

None of his friends said a word, but Hasan went to great efforts to prove that this theory was wrong.

"The truth is," Ibrahim Khairat said, "none of our old revolutions achieved any startling results. Now this revolution has come along to fulfill the missions of the old ones as well as achieve its own particular goals."

The conversation continued until the house was empty. When Isa went to see Hasan to the door, the latter stopped suddenly and smiled at him fondly. "Your trip was a mistake," he said. "You should examine your position again."

Isa smiled. He had not the least inclination to talk.

"Tell me one of your past hopes," Hasan continued, "which hasn't been achieved today. You should jump on the train and join the rest of us!"

Isa shook his head enigmatically. They shook hands.

"When you change your mind," Hasan said, "you'll find me at your beck and call."

Isa thanked him gratefully. In fact, he was greatly touched by his kindness, but he refused to think about moving that wall which kept them apart. He often admitted his adversary's logic and acknowledged his own secret defeat in front of him. But every time he seemed more convinced, he felt a bitter resentment building up inside him.

Afterwards, he sat down with Umm Shalabi, who greeted his arrival with a flood of tears over the death of his late mother. He waited till she quieted down. "How was she?" he asked.

"She didn't sleep for a single day."

"Suddenly then?"

"Yes, and, fortunately, in my arms."

"Was she alone in the house for a long time?"

"Never. One of your sisters came to see her every day."

"Didn't Susan Hanem come tonight?"

"Yes, sir, she did."

"And Salwa?" he asked after a short pause.

"No, sir, she didn't come." She blinked and then continued. "She's engaged to your cousin Hasan . . ."

His weary eyes leapt in a look of astonishment. "Salwa and Hasan?"

"Yes, sir."

"Since when?"

"Last month."

He stretched out his legs carelessly and leaned back against the headrest of his chair. He saw the old, faded ceiling resting on its horizontal pillars. His gaze settled on a large gecko at the top of the wall; it was so still that it seemed to be crucified there.

NINETEEN

It was nice to sit on the El Bodega pavement in the warm June air, especially when the evening brought with it a gentle breeze. Silence prevailed when a pretty girl walked by, but Isa and his friends were by no means tired of talking about politics. Even though Abbas Sadiq had a position in the government, and Ibrahim Khairat worked as a lawyer and writer for the revolution, they still held the same views as Isa or Samir Abd al-Baqi, who tended to be reticent. Ibrahim summed up their general feelings. "It's right there in your hands, and then someone else gets it!" he said.

Signs of resignation were written all over their faces, but they still hoped for a miracle. Sometimes they would seize on the most trivial news, and a hidden flicker of life would rouse in the barren wasteland of their hearts. Incredibly enough, Ibrahim Khairat and Abbas Sadiq were even more disgruntled than Isa.

"One of you is an important writer," Isa told them with a laugh, "and the other is an important civil servant. So what do you want?"

"On a personal level," Abbas replied in his ringing and harmonious voice, his eyes flashing wide, "things may be reassuring; but that doesn't alter the general picture."

"The truth is," said Ibrahim Khairat, "no one has any value today, however senior his position may be. We're a country of bubbles."

"When I was only in the sixth grade," Abbas said, "I was as good as an entire ministry!"

"Nothing bothers me anymore," said Samir Abd al-Baqi with a soothing tone of resignation.

"But your position is at least as difficult as any of ours!"

Samir hurriedly revised his statement of his views. "I meant that I'm no longer troubled by regrets about the past. Sometimes I wish them success. My own dismissal doesn't bother me because I chose it."

"You mean, it was imposed on you," said Isa jokingly.

"But, at the same time, I chose it. May God's will be done."

Ibrahim Khairat rubbed Isa's shoulder. "Why aren't you saying anything?" he asked. "Haven't you any news?"

"A few days ago," Isa said simply, "I hung a 'For Sale' sign on my late mother's house."

"It's old, but at least it's land!"

"My share of it will enable me to live like a notable," Isa said joyfully, "and that's how I'll carry on for as long as possible."

"Do you think that's a decent way to live?"

"Maybe it'll cure me of my split personality."

"Is that some modern illness?" asked Abbas Sadiq.

"The truth is," replied Isa after thinking for a moment, "although my mind is sometimes convinced by the revolution, my heart is always with the past. I just don't know if there can be any settlement between the two."

"It isn't a question of principles to be convinced by," said Ibrahim Khairat. "The relationship between ruler and ruled is regulated secretly, just as in love. We can say that the ruler who will be most attractive to his subjects is the one who respects their humanity the most. Man shall not live by bread alone!"

"But that's why I would still be out of work, even if I got scores of jobs," Isa replied sadly.

"Is that your heart or your mind speaking?" Abbas Sadiq asked.

"The heart means totally different things to us," Samir Abd al-Baqi said with a smile.

"Why are we laughing," Isa asked, "when life is a tragedy in every sense of the word?"

"We think of death as the ultimate tragedy," said Ibrahim Khairat, "and yet the death of the living is infinitely worse than that of the dead."

Abbas Sadiq gave an explosive laugh. "Isn't it appropriate," he said, "that the conversation should take us from death to the atom!"

Isa had still not fully emerged from his sudden feeling of sorrow. "One of the things about using the atom as a threat," he said, "is that it lightens life's drudgery; I mean, our life . . ."

"What about modern civilization?" Abbas Sadiq asked sarcastically. "Aren't you worried about what may happen to it?"

"Fortunately for us, we haven't entered the world of modern civilization yet. So why should we be afraid of getting wet?"

"I hope it'll be an age like the flood," Ibrahim Khairat said. "Then the earth will be purified."

"Have you heard that from an official source?" Abbas Sadiq asked.

"Let's admit," said Samir Abd al-Baqi, "that if it weren't for death, our life wouldn't have any value at all."

"What a lot of talk about death!"

At that, Isa remembered his mother's death, Salwa's marriage to Hasan, and the harsh way he had treated Riri. How consoling it was, he thought, to be able to chat with these friends of his. Talking to Hasan only made his split personality even more acute. Samir leaned toward him. "Your problem's easy compared with the problems of the world," he said. "You need a job and a wife."

"That's why I like horror films," Isa replied with no obvious connection.

"The trouble with those films," Abbas Sadiq commented, "is that they're imaginary."

"On the contrary," Isa replied, "the trouble with them is that they're too realistic."

The air-raid siren went off by mistake and blared for half a minute. Isa thought that eventually he would find himself searching for a job and a woman. But that would not happen till he admitted defeat and made a final exit from history.

TWENTY

The pleasures of the night are very intense, but they do not last long; and besides, they cost too much. The Arizona was particularly beautiful at midnight; gorgeous girls of various nationalities were dancing around, and drinks were mingled with the early morning dew. You could make do with lies. In the back garden, it was all love and lovers, moonlight or starlight. Money had no value at all, and emotions spilled over unchecked. There's nothing new about the picture, Isa thought, but he was still maintaining the deceits of his daily life in a fearsomely dull atmosphere. Here, on the other hand, you could blend in with the singing in a joyful ambience. Salwa had known about luxury, but she had never really known joy. It occurred to him to ask his Italian companion in the garden a question. "You've been to a number of countries; what do you think of people?"

She was something for all five senses to enjoy. "They're usually looking for pleasure when I meet them," she replied, "so they're all very nice!"

"But that's all lies."

"At least they're genuine about wanting me!"

"That's just a passing emotion."

"Everything's like that!"

He laughed and paused for a moment. "Can't you find even that passing emotion in yourself?" he asked.

"So you don't believe I love you?" she asked jokingly.

"How is it," he asked her with interest, "that it doesn't occur to people like you to enjoy a little stability in your lives?"

She sang an Italian song, and for a moment he was impressed by her beauty. Then his own degradation made him feel sad. Everything of value except beauty comes to the same end, he thought; people barter shamelessly with freedom, humanity, and even religion, and they are all really a single tragedy. In the past, he himself had indulged in this futile pastime. He had stomached all kinds of corruption and taken part in it himself; his bank balance was still there to prove it. Why couldn't purity prevail? What was it that had prevented it for so many centuries? Was there a single man anywhere on the face of the earth living without fear or blemish?

He began to amuse himself by following girls in the Cairo streets, especially young ones; it was as though some force were pushing him toward the sources of innocence. But these were mysterious and fruitless trips which brought no results. Every time the political storms blew up, and some idea or person from his past was thrown out, he reeled under the impact of the blow. Eventually there came a time when he wished that the Egyptians—like some other peoples—had a colony, in South America perhaps, where they could emigrate. The Egyptians were reptiles, he told himself angrily, not birds. The dream of some radical change in his life attracted him, but everything he did was just a waste of time. When he complained to his friend Samir Abd al-Baqi, his friend had replied, "Where's your sail? You're a boat drifting without a sail!"

One day at about four in the afternoon, the real estate agent came to say that some people wanted to look at the house. Two women appeared, an old lady in her seventies, and her daughter—at least that was what he deduced from their resemblance—who was in her forties or slightly younger. He took them from one room to another and answered their questions. The old lady was thin, with a white complexion, gray eyes, and thick eyebrows, and her expression full of experience and self-confidence. Her daughter was of medium height and had a full figure and a round face; her eyes were like those of a cow and equally placid. He noticed the women's amazement at the obvious discrepancy between the old house and the magnificent, contemporary furniture. This irritated him. After they had looked at the large court-yard, he invited them to sit in the reception room and offered them some coffee. The agent joined the group, and in his white *gallabiyya** looked at everyone with his narrow eyes. "The house covers a large area," he said, "and one could add a building on two sides. The northwest corner is a magnifi-cent site; the quarter around it is rapidly being modernized, as you've seen. Five new buildings are being erected at the same time, and that'll raise its value."

"But the house is old," said the daughter. Isa again noticed her black eyes and elegant clothes. "It's not fit to live in."

"You're not buying a house to live in, of course," Isa said. "It's a site to build on, as Al-Hajj* Husain just pointed out. It's a good location, and the price is right. You can make your own inquiries and find out for yourself!"

"And that's just the present," Al-Hajj Husain continued. "The entire quarter's guaranteed for the future as well. There's no quarter in the world like this one; it's in a perfect location, there are so many people living here, and transpor-tation is good—it's ideal."

The daughter asked Isa about the dimensions of the prop-erty. She had a guttural voice that was rounded like her face, but provocative at the same time. Her magnificent appearance indicated to him that she was a woman who deserved some respect; she might be quite desirable too, for a while.

"A thousand square meters," he replied. "Al-Hajj Husain may have told you the price I'm asking."

"Ten thousand pounds!" the old lady exclaimed. "Where will you find someone to pay that much?!"

"Here!" Isa replied, pointing at her with a laugh.

"It's the kind of opportunity the world doesn't offer twice," Al-Hajj Husain said emphatically. "God be my witness!"

Isa refused to consider lowering the price a single piaster. The bargaining went on interminably, but it foundered on his determination. During all this haggling Isa and the daughter exchanged probing glances which had nothing at all to do with business. He got the impression that she was not married, and told himself that she was rich and acceptable. She was not the type he liked, it was true, and they were not the same age, but she was wealthy, placid, and well mannered, as far as he could tell. These were just passing notions, but it struck him that the old lady was following his train of thought. The meeting came to end without his changing his mind or the old lady accepting his price.

TWENTY-ONE

The agent advised him to do a bit of bargaining, but he felt a pressing need to make his future secure and so he refused. His share of the selling price of the house would enable him to maintain his present standard of living for ten years at least, and during that long period of time a suitable job might open up for him. None of his three sisters disagreed with the position he had taken, and he was given absolute freedom to accept or reject the offer.

Days went by and he began to get worried. Then the agent brought him the good news that the lady had accepted the quoted price. From the agent's chatter he gathered that Inayat Hanem was the widow of a police officer, but her money had been left to her by her father. Her daughter, Qadriyya, her only child, had been divorced five years earlier without ever having any children. Isa went to visit the lady at home in a building she owned in Sakakini Square.* The superb, classically styled furniture showed that the family had real prestige, and all the formalities of the sale were settled at a friendly session. Isa pointed to the picture of the lady's husband. "I knew your late husband," he said suavely. "When I first started working, I heard enough things about him to convince me that he was a respectable man and loved his homeland."

This had a very good effect on the two women. Inayat Hanem invited him to stay for a while, and before long the servant brought in some tea and splendid cakes. The old woman expressed her happiness at being able to serve as hostess to one of her late husband's admirers. However, Isa did not sense that his welcome was due to any generosity on her part, and guessed that the invitation was rather more for her daughter's benefit. Qadriyya was sitting quietly and filled up the empty chair very nicely; from time to time, she looked at him drowsily.

"Those days serving in the provinces were really unforgettable," Inayat Hanem said, "days full of goodness. My late husband earned Saad Zaghlul's esteem, and he was transferred to the Interior in 1924. But he was subjected to the worst kinds of treatment during the periods of revolution." She went on to praise his intuition. "When Qadriyya's husband came to ask for her hand," she told Isa to prove her point, "my late husband said he was not happy with him. But I insisted, and so I was responsible for my daughter's bad luck!"

Isa happily took his cue. "How was that, might I ask?"

"He was from a good family, but had a really depraved character. My daughter is a good girl; she looks after the house, and is of a generous disposition. By her very nature, she wasn't prepared when he turned her home into a tavern and gaming den!"

"What bad luck!" Isa said regretfully. "Our Lord will recompense her well for her patience."

A considerable amount of time passed in this heavily loaded conversation. Isa asked himself how much he could enjoy a woman like Qadriyya; he could regard her as a kind of lifetime security, and she could undoubtedly be considered a stroke of good fortune when measured against the misfortunes he had suffered.

When he left the house, he was sure that he had made a considerable impression on the two women. Qadriyya needs a husband, he thought with a good deal of sorrow, and I need a wife. He decided to make a few of the usual inquiries, which established that she had been married three times, not just once. The first had lasted for only a month. She had been betrothed to a relative of her father's, and before the marriage was consummated, they had realized that he was after her money and was just taking advantage of her. Her father had forced him to divorce her. The second had lasted for four or five years. Her mother was not prepared to give her daughter any of her money, even though the husband had asked that she should and kept pressing her. She thought that he should be able to take care of his own responsibilities without any help from her, and that these requests were irresponsible and showed some sinister design on his part. The argument had ended in divorce. The third marriage had lasted for six years and seemed likely to last, especially since her mother had changed her policy and gave her enough money and more. But the husband had wanted children, and Qadriyya had given him none; and judging from her previous marriage, probably would never do so. The husband had married again in secret and then told her. This had caused a crisis which could not continue indefinitely and so she was divorced for the third time.

This, then, was Qadriyya's story. However, Isa did not go into all the details in the corner at El Bodega. "A very presentable woman wants to marry me!" he said.

Their gazes fastened on him like compass needles attracted to a pole.

"She's from a very respectable and wealthy family," he said gleefully and with a touch of vanity.

"The last quality you mentioned is the one to look for!" said Abbas Sadiq with his ringing voice, as though he were announcing the news.

"I hope you'll be very happy," said Ibrahim Khairat, smiling to hide his jealous feelings. "We should see about repairing the house now that political hurricanes are about to knock it down!"

This bitter comment irritated him. "Particularly as I haven't got a pen to use to curry favor with my enemies!" he retorted.

They all laughed. He was inundated with questions and began to answer them cautiously until the lies were piling up. He only revealed his real feelings to Samir Abd al-Baqi as they were walking alone together down Sulaiman Pasha Street. He told him the whole, unadulterated truth.

"Aren't you concerned about having children?" Samir asked.

"I need to find a companion and put an end to my loneliness," Isa responded angrily. "This woman is quite respectable and she's prepared to take me with all my faults. So why shouldn't I accept her with hers? Where can I find a decent girl who'll accept me in my present circumstances?"

He went to see Inayat Hanem to ask for Qadriyya's hand, and found her quite prepared to accept his proposal. "I want to be honest with you," he said. "Lies are the enemy of marriage. I have a fair amount of money left in the bank, in addition to my share of the money on the sale of the house. I also have a small pension. At the moment, I haven't got a job, but it's possible that I'll find a decent job in the future. I was expelled from the government, not for reasons having to do with honor but because of blind political partisanship. It wasn't possible for the present regime to spare someone like me whom it regards as being very dangerous!"

"That's fine," the old lady replied. "We're not worried about money. We prefer work only because it's undesirable to be doing nothing. I've no doubts about your honor whatsoever; my late husband suffered just as you have. My heart tells me that you'll be the best husband for my daughter."

She did not tell him about her daughter's successive marriages or her sterility. That made him happy. He realized that, if he knew about the bride's faults in advance, later on he wouldn't be able to play the role of the faithful husband whose hopes have been dashed. And that was a very important role to leave open should he later have the chance to regain his influence and prestige!

TWENTY-TWO

He travelled to Ra's al-Barr* to spend his honeymoon in Inayat Hanem's chalet. Relations among the three of them grew
in a way which augured well for the future. From the beginning, he wanted to be a man in every sense of the word. He
did not give way on anything which he felt he might regret
later on. For that reason, he refused to stay in her mother's
house, even though she suggested it, and insisted on living
with his wife far away in Dokki, that quarter with its unforgettable memories. He showed a strange courage in telling
her quite frankly that they both—he and his wife, that is—
had to enjoy her money while she was alive so that they
could honestly wish her a long life! He was sticking to his
demands till they were all met in full; the reason why the
mighty party had been ruined, he told himself, was that it
had been too tolerant toward the end of its life, a life which
had otherwise been marked by an obstinate persistence.

He was seeing Ra's al-Barr for the first time in his life. He
was struck by its special character, the way it combined the
beauties of the city, the countryside, and the shore. The place
where the Nile and the sea came together fascinated him, and
so did the all-embracing quiet, like some happy dream, the
fresh faces, and the dry, gentle breeze which seemed somehow to infringe on the house's sanctity as it permeated the
hospitable walls. He did not find any of his friends on a summer vacation, and so he devoted all his time to his family.
He found his marriage a great success and felt he had a powerful influence over his wife. For the first time, he found it
irksome to be idle once he discovered that life in the house

was revolving around an axis other than his own. He found out that neither his personality nor his wife's love of him, nor the way in which his mother-in-law adapted to his wishes, could drive this painful feeling away. In the old days, he had openly lived like a notable with his money, but now everyone was looking at his wife and her money.

No one would believe that he could lead a life of luxury forever with his share from the sale of the house and his pension. He started hiding his thoughts behind loud laughter and a pretense of naïveté and trust. However, he was quite sure that his life would not go on like this for long, and that he had to arouse his dormant ambitions and embark upon some enterprise worthy of himself.

He learned everything about his wife by living with her. She emerged as a past master at cooking and making clothes. She filled him up with different kinds of food, especially sweetmeats, which she was particularly good at making. She was gluttonous and infected the people with whom she ate with the same vice. Her prowess at innocent games like backgammon and conquian* gave her a great deal of pleasure. She was a devotee of the cinema and the comic theater even though her primary education had been almost completely erased from her memory; all she retained of it was a meager ability to read and to write a poor letter. A woman in every sense of the word, she had a fiery temperament, allowing him no complaints on that score. However, he did worry about the way she jumped down his throat every time she could. It seemed that she had an unconscious desire to make a husband, father, and son out of him at one and the same time; this may have had something to do with her sad but overwhelming longing for children, and the way she expressed her suppressed emotions through worried looks and sudden nervous movements that did not suit her staid and ample person. Misery, Isa thought, seems to be the greatest common denominator among people everywhere; and then he thought how insignificant appearances really are. What could be the hidden reason for this absurdity? he wondered; it is fortunate that we can at least hide our thoughts from other people. I wonder what ideas about me are going around in that small head of hers covered with thick hair. Would she be upset, for example, if she knew the real reasons for my having to give up my post?

He thought of Salwa and the wound she had gouged in his heart, and felt even more unnerved. He thought of Riri as well; he frowned bitterly, and a black look came over his face. He was aware of his own limitless insignificance, and recalled how the ministry used to quake when he got out of his government Chevrolet in the morning. He also remembered a day when he had wanted to put himself forward as a candidate for the Al-Wayiliyya district. But Abd al-Halim Pasha Shukri had advised him to hold off till the coming elections because he was sure that he would be nominated as under secretary in the ministry!

One day, the radio surprised him by announcing the nationalization of the Suez Canal Company. His interest rose to boiling point, and he started panting apprehensively as in the old days. Before long, he was immersed in the same enthusiasm which was engulfing everyone. He longed to see his absent friends so that he could discuss the situation with them. He acknowledged in a daze that it was something of almost unbelievable significance and importance, and there his mind stopped. His heart buried itself inside him like an invalid, and a feeling of jealousy gnawed away at him. He felt alarmed every time a peak was reached in the present which would compare with those peaks in history which served as the backcloth for his life's memories. He felt an intense pain as he experienced the tug-of-war between the two sides of his own split personality. He wondered what the consequences might be, and tried to ask himself what his stand was in relation to them. But he soon fled from this inner struggle by sharing the news with his wife and her mother. However, he found they had no reaction to the events, and he hurried to the refrigerator to get something to drink.

In the middle of September, he returned to Cairo with his senses bloated. He had noticeably gained weight. He walked past his old home on his way to his new house in Dokki, and sad memories came flooding back. All his friends now had young, educated wives, and he began to exchange visits with them. Qadriyya was especially admired because of her social standing and wealth. Samir Abd al-Baqi asked him how he liked married life.

"It's fine," he replied after a diplomatic pause, "but . . ."

"But?"

"I doubt if any man could stand it without a job or children."

The Jews attacked Sinai. The papers slapped that in his face one morning, and the news staggered him. He sat down by the radio and followed the news with dwindling attention; it had such an effect on him that he was almost babbling. Thoughts spun around inside his head till he felt dizzy. Yes indeed, he thought, the fate of the revolution is swaying in the balance. However, his own nationalist feelings burst out and overwhelmed everything else; he showed a rage worthy of an old nationalist almost overtaken by death, an old nationalist who was suffering even though he had been tarnished because of Egypt. His feet clung to the edge of the abyss which threatened to annihilate his own country. He pushed the revolution and its fate out of his mind so that he could keep his feelings completely responsive. Through the sheer force of his will, he eliminated those contradictory emotions which were spreading beneath the stream of his turbulent consciousness. Turning toward his wife, he was astonished to see how unconcerned she seemed and how completely she was bound up in the routine of her daily life. She only came out of it when she asked scornfully, "War and raids again?"

He treated the whole thing as a joke and teased her to calm his nerves. "You're very concerned about getting food ready," he said. "Tell me, how would the world be if everyone behaved like you?"

"Wars would stop!" she replied simply.

In spite of his anxiety, he managed to laugh. "Qadriyya, you're not worried about public affairs," he said, feeling the urge to make a joke. "I mean things involving the people and our country."

"It's enough for me to look after you and your home."

"Don't you love Egypt?"

"Of course!"

"Don't you want our Army to win?"

"Of course. Then we'll have some peace again."

"But don't you even want to think about it?"

"I've got quite enough to worry about."

"Tell me how you would feel if the Jews were trying to take over your mother's property!"

"What a terrible thought," she replied with a laugh. "Have we killed any of them?"

He found it all very amusing, and it helped to relieve his tense feelings. Even though the sky was very overcast, they went to visit Inayat Hanem in Sakakini and had lunch with her. They left before it got dark. They were standing in the square looking for a taxi when the siren went off. She gripped his arm. "Let's go back," she whispered in a shaky voice.

They returned to her mother's building. As they were climbing the stairs, an antiaircraft gun began firing. She shuddered and his heart jumped violently. They all gathered in a room with the blinds closed.

"From one war to the next," Inayat Hanem protested, "life is lost. Sirens, antiaircraft guns, bombs. Wouldn't it be a good idea for us to seek refuge in another country?"

They stayed there in the darkness with dry throats. Four guns boomed out in the distance.

"This generation will enter paradise without any Day of Reckoning!" her mother continued.

How could the Jews dare to attack Egypt, Isa asked himself in despair, when she had prepared herself with such an army?

TWENTY-THREE

The next evening he rushed to El Bodega with his head full of comforting and encouraging news from the newspapers. The weather was really marvelous as they clustered together around the table on the pavement. A warm and powerful force drew them all together, a force restless with the combined feelings of danger and hope. Ibrahim Khairat drew his small frame up to its full height. "Do you think," he asked excitedly, "that Israel will just make this one move?"

They looked at one another in a strange way which expressed their inner feelings clearly, as though some kind of drunkenness had put them all into a daze.

"France, England, and America are all behind Israel," Ibrahim Khairat continued.

Isa wondered anxiously how he could define his own position in the midst of such turbulent thoughts and emotions as these.

"It looks as though our army will be finished," said Samir Abd al-Baqi, "before our allies declare themselves."

They all laughed. The evening brought with it a quiet and secrecy. Ibrahim Khairat lowered his voice. "Things are clear now," he said. "This is the end!"

They listened to him with a sense of nervous joy, and some of them even felt a little guilt. Abbas Sadiq raised his head from the *nargila*. His bulging eyes were gleaming brightly. "They have supporters behind them too," he said.

"No one could be so crazy," said Ibrahim Khairat scornfully, "as to think seriously that a world war is going to flare up over a spot which can hardly be seen on the world map."

Isa found that their feelings reflected some of what he himself was thinking. He decided, however, that the other side of it should be voiced. "Do you really want the Jews to defeat us?" he asked.

"There will be a superficial defeat," Ibrahim Khairat said, "which will rid us of the new occupation army. Then Israel will be forced to retreat and maybe even to be satisfied with taking over Sinai and making peace with the Arabs. England and France will intervene to settle the problems connected with the Near East and return things to normal in Egypt."

"Doesn't that mean a reversion to Western influence?" Isa asked.

"That's better than the present situation, at any rate."

"What a trap we've fallen into!" said Isa, as though he were talking to himself. "We stumble about, then we're torn to pieces, and finally we suffer terribly. We betray either our homeland or ourselves. However, from my point of view, a defeat in this particular war would be worse than death."

"You're very romantic," Abbas Sadiq said.

"Why should we be unhappy?" Ibrahim Khairat asked. "There's nothing left to be unhappy about, and, in a dead man's view, any kind of life is better than death."

"Sometimes," Isa replied, "I tell myself that death would be more bearable than going backwards, and at other times I tell myself that it would be better to remain without a role in a country which has one, rather than to have a role in a country which has none."

"By your own admission," said Ibrahim Khairat with a smile, "you've got a split personality. We're not concerned about the side of you which is talking; the opinion of the silent side is good enough for us!"

They all laughed loudly. It was getting dark. Ibrahim Khairat looked at Samir Abd al-Baqi as if to urge him to say something.

"I would like all our fellow citizens to live to enjoy human generosity," said Samir.

"So you agree with us, do you?" Ibrahim Khairat asked.

"My words have a more profound significance than that," Samir replied tersely.

"Are you opposed to our views then?"

"My words have a more profound significance than that," he repeated.

Isa was lost in his own troubled thoughts. The side of him which was speaking had to defeat the silent side. He had to help it out; he had to show his scorn for the assailant quite shamelessly and thereby show his scorn for the silent side of himself. What has led us to this really sorry state of affairs? he wondered. Was there no way to forget personal defeats? The disease was raging throughout the country.

The air-raid siren sounded like a wall collapsing on them suddenly. All light left the world, and the street was filled with the sound of people running in the dark. Samir suggested they go inside the café, but the idea got no encouragement from anyone. Isa thought of his wife on her own in Dokki with Umm Shalabi and felt sorry for her. Suddenly they were frightened by the sound of distant explosions, coming one after another. They quickly hurried into the café to the corner where they sat in the winter. The distant blasts kept coming with a frightening regularity. People started guessing in what parts of town they were falling. Shubra? Heliopolis? Hulwan?

"Where did the Jews get such forces?"

"And where are our planes?"

The attack continued and was certainly severe enough to be termed a real raid. The country had probably seen nothing like it throughout the Second World War. Their nerves were really on edge. A man came rushing in from outside. "It's

British planes that are dropping the bombs!" he said in a voice which the whole blacked-out café could hear.

"Impossible!" scores of people yelled.

"I heard it on the Near East station!" he replied to confirm the news.

Comments began to pour out like hallucinations. Then the bombing stopped. Minutes passed in an anxious silence, and then the all-clear siren sounded. They released themselves from the grip of tension, and as the lights came on, gazed at each other with the same look of bewilderment that covers your face when you wake up after a long sleep. They were deciding whether to go or stay when the air-raid siren sounded again. Before long the explosions started again.

"The end seems even nearer than we thought," Ibrahim Khairat whispered.

"Pray God we're not a part of it," Samir Abd al-Baqi whispered.

After an hour of torture, the all-clear siren sounded. They left the café quickly and got into Ibrahim Khairat's car. They had only just gotten to Abu Ala's bridge when the siren sounded for the third time. They stopped the car near the pavement. As there were no shelters nearby, they decided to stay in the car. "We've got to live!" Ibrahim Khairat said with a nervous laugh. "The price of stock in our lives keeps going up."

About an hour later, they heard the all-clear siren. The Ford sped across the bridge, and then crossed the Zamalek Bridge headed for Sharia an-Nil. Just as the start of it, the air-raid siren sounded for a fourth time. They stopped the car near an open space. The raid continued and the bombing was heavy.

"Maybe they're bombing particular targets," Isa said to calm himself.

"Maybe they're bombing at random," said Samir anxiously.

"Bombing civilians is a terrible responsibility in the face of world opinion," Abbas Sadiq said in a voice which sounded as though he had been hit by shrapnel himself.

"The best thing is to keep calm," Ibrahim Khairat said.

The all-clear siren sounded half an hour later. The car sped along at top speed to get them home before the air-raid siren came on again.

TWENTY-FOUR

The Cairo sky was crisscrossed with planes day and night. The incredible thing was that daily life in houses, offices, shops, and markets carried on as usual, even though planes were screaming incessantly overhead and explosions kept going off. People still thought that the bombs were not falling indiscriminately, but there were many rumors of casualties. They carried on as usual, but death was looking down at them from a nearby window; its harbingers flew into their cars and it intruded into their innermost thoughts. The city was turned into an army camp; convoys of armored vehicles and trucks moved along the streets, and normal life was drowned in a sea of thoughts and misgivings.

Inayat Hanem came to live with her daughter in Dokki till things settled down. At night, the world looked as it had before history. They gathered around the radio in the house; their mouths felt very dry and they hoped that listening to the voices of the announcers and the national songs would help to relieve the dryness.

The explosions and gunfire carried on like street vendors' cries. Eventually the old lady's eyes began to wander and lost their color. She clutched the rosary in her palm as though it were a lightning conductor. Qadriyya broke down as quickly as her mother, and her robustness was of no help to her. Her languid eyes lost their look of majestic apathy. The discussions at the United Nations emerged from the radio like air for a suffocating man. The tales from Port Said followed and they began to grieve.

"Can we stand up to the English and French?" Qadriyya asked in a moment of alarm.

"Port Said is fighting back," Isa replied anxiously, "and the world's in a state of revolution!"

"They're all talking, and we're being hit!"

"Yes. What can be done?"

"There has to be a solution," she shouted nervously, "any solution. If there isn't, my nerves will be destroyed."

His nerves were on the verge of collapse too. Sadness, darkness, and prison. The darkness inspired him to hope desperately for victory. Many things melted away in the darkness. He forgot about the past and the future, and focused on the desire for victory. Perhaps the fact that he could not leave the house gave him a better chance to think about the situation and become thoroughly aware of the danger, to yearn for victory and keep the hidden side of his own nature quiet. Deep down inside him, a well of enthusiasm began to move which almost pushed him toward self-sacrifice. As he dawdled around in the daytime, he could read in hundreds of other faces the same feelings which tied him to life in spite of all the dust, oblivion, and undercurrents of selfishness. He was like a drowning man, thinking only of saving himself. It seemed to him that the barrier which stood between him and the revolution was dissolving at a rate which he would never have thought possible before.

Ibrahim Khairat came to visit him one afternoon on his way to his office in the city. He seemed extremely self-confident and serious. "The whole tragedy will be over in a few hours," he said.

Isa looked at him in bewilderment with his big, round eyes.

"Some of our men are meeting the responsible authorities at this moment," said Ibrahim. He was frowning because he felt a sense of authority. "We're trying to persuade them to surrender so that we can save whatever can be saved!"

Isa got the impression that he was seeing the High Commissioner's procession just as he had done in the old days. "What's left to be saved?" he asked.

"Don't be overly pessimistic," Ibrahim retorted, and then continued angrily: "People who regard life and death as the same thing are really miserable creatures."

"It's like a nightmare," Isa said sorrowfully.

"With the state of mind we're in," said Ibrahim angrily, "defeat is easy to live with."

"We'd soon get tired if we started counting mankind's troubles. I'm asking myself whether life is really fit for human beings!"

Ibrahim Khairat shrugged his shoulders contemptuously.

"Maybe it's some sort of idiocy to hang on to life in spite of all its miseries," Isa continued. "But as long as we're alive, we should wage an unflagging war on all types of stupidity."

"Tell me," Ibrahim asked him, "have you really changed?"

Isa did not say a word, but his face contracted into an expression of utter disgust. However, when the crisis reached its peak, new factors came rushing into the whirlpool. The world gave its decision, the threats disappeared, and the enemy was forced to swallow his pride and submit to an unprecedented reality. Then there was an outburst of joy greater than any bomb.

Life returned to the corner in El Bodega, and the friends all met again. A faded smile, and a languid look which could not see into the future.

"There's some hope that we'll gain some weight," said Ibrahim Khairat mockingly, "like people who are condemned to death!"

Abbas Sadiq brandished the stem of his *nargila*. "This is a chance," he said, "which is a million times rarer than winning money at roulette."

Even Samir Abd al-Baqi's green eyes showed signs of disappointment deep down. Even more remarkable was the fact that Isa himself—even after he had felt the taste of victory —rapidly sank into a profound lethargy like a pile of ash. His thoughts turned in on themselves and were buried in darkness once more.

TWENTY-FIVE

Everyone has a job, but he had none. Every wife has children, but she had none. Every citizen in a country has his own abode, but he was an exile in his own homeland. After the usual escapist roles, what was left? In the mornings, he daw-dled from one café to another; in the evenings, he would mull over his sorrows at El Bodega and make boring visits within the family circle. After the usual escapist roles, what was left? He went through terrible agonies, and felt lonely and bored. How much longer can this miserable existence last? he asked himself.

There he was sitting by the windowpane, sunning himself in the bitter cold, jobless and hopeless. Qadriyya was con-centrating on some crocheting. She no longer dispelled his feeling of loneliness. With her disheveled hair and swollen features, she showed all the signs of an all too common ne-glect. She had become fatter and fleshier, and her face showed clearly that in its natural state it was a complete stranger to the comeliness of youth.

He looked at her sorrowfully, and then turned away to read the headlines in the papers; he no longer bothered to read the news. Then he gave up and started talking to him-self; in recent years he had been doing a great deal of this. Qadriyya was not the wife he had been looking for, and he still felt bitterly sorry about Salwa, even though the love itself had died long since. If it had not been for the wine, he would not have been able to give himself up to Qadriyya's arms. Nor would he have tolerated the hints about her wealth, which she kept using to hem him in, if it were not for the utter despair which he felt. It was pure agony for him every time he remembered that she was spending money on her home while he was not spending a penny of his pension, except, that is, on himself. Even his bank balance did him no good at all in his family life. So what was the point of all this sponging?

One day, she proved to him that she too was thinking about other things besides mealtimes and crocheting. "Isa," she said, "you seem very distracted, and sometimes you look so miserable. It makes me very worried."

Isa said that he was sorry that she was worried. "I'm quite well," he continued, "so don't worry yourself about that."

"Some things can be harmful for a man."

"Such as?"

"Not working when he can."

He smiled even though he was really furious. "Maybe you're annoyed," he said, "to find your husband out of a job."

"It doesn't worry me at all," she replied emphatically, "apart from the effect which it has on you."

"What do you suggest I do?"

"You know best about that, my dear."

"There aren't any ministerial posts vacant at the moment," he replied simply.

They both laughed with no feeling at all. However, she carried on hopefully. "Think about it seriously," she said. "Please."

He told himself that she was right, and that she did occasionally have a sensible idea in that stupid head of hers. He himself was convinced that he needed to get a job, but why did his ambition let him down? Did his will have some kind of disease? Why didn't he open an office, or else join one?

He was thinking about a job, but living without one and

without any serious initiative about taking the required step. His bank balance gave him a certain amount of security, and this had been increased by his prosperous marriage. And apart from all that, his pension could cover his daily expenses. So he gave in to laziness and arrogance, and his eternal sense of alienation was too great to let him begin at the bottom of the ladder. He sought consolation in any way he could, at home or outside, in Ra's al-Barr* or Alexandria, without paying any attention to the passage of time.

"You're getting heavier all the time," Samir Abd al-Baqi told him. "You should look after yourself."

It was true that he was eating too much, sweets especially, and no meal went by without his having a glass or two. "I'm quite aware of that," he replied. "People will say that my wife is fattening me up well."

"I was only thinking of your health," replied Samir timidly.

"Yes, I daresay," said Isa. "But sometimes I can read it in people's eyes."

"It's entirely your own fault," said Samir with a frown. "You're so lazy. I often wonder in amazement where that Isa who used to leave the ministry after midnight almost every day has disappeared to, to say nothing of the one who put so much into the party and the club."

One day, the radio announcer spoke about the space flight and the dawning of a new era. Isa woke up from his slumber, and a new interest intruded into his apathetic spirit. He started reading the papers avidly again and listening closely to the radio. The corner in El Bodega found something else to do apart from talking about political misfortunes and chewing over rumors.

"Isn't it marvelous," Abbas Sadiq remarked, "to read the papers every morning with this feeling of excitement?"

"This marks the setting of the politicians' star," said Ibra-him Khairat maliciously. "Why don't they relinquish their positions to the *ulama** and then go to blazes?"

"Now we should start looking hopefully to the heavens again!" said Samir Abd al-Baqi.

Isa raised his eyes to the ceiling as though he were looking at the heavens, and pictured the stars and planets to himself with a childlike desire for some magical and imaginary means of escape. "How wonderful it would be to leave the earth forever," he muttered, and then continued complaining. "It's all become so boring, it's like a disease!"

He wondered if it would be possible for him to establish his connection with mankind in general and to forget his compulsory affiliation with this country.

TWENTY-SIX

They all spent the summer at Ra's al-Barr, which was in itself
unusual; even Abbas Sadiq, a devotee of Alexandria, was
there. Ibrahim Khairat got a room ready in his chalet where
they could play cards and drink, and they all went back there
after their regular exercise on the banks of the Nile. Shaikh
Abd at-Tawwab as-Salhubi was on vacation at the same time
and joined up with them. Isa slid into poker with no trouble
at all; the gambling and the fact that it kept him up till dawn
led to his first serious quarrel with Qadriyya. When there
was a quarrel, he found that she could be as stubborn as a
mule. But he did not care and carried on scornfully in his
own sweet way. When he took his place at the table, Ibrahim
Khairat poured him out a glass of cognac and asked how
things were going at home.

"Lousy," Isa replied tersely.

"Our wives are more tolerant than Qadriyya Hanem,"
commented Abbas Sadiq. "She shouldn't keep such a close
watch on you in a beautiful haven like Ra's al-Barr."

Isa looked at his hand and was delighted to see he had a
pair of aces. He entered the round with high hopes, and then
luck gave him a pair of eights. He won six piasters.

"Just look after your profits," said Shaikh As-Salhubi with
a smile, "and things will get better at home!"

"His wife's not worried about money," Abbas Sadiq said
to put things straight.

The remark was quite spontaneous, but it hurt Isa very
much, particularly as he was usually unlucky at card games;

so much so that he had had to withdraw a hundred pounds from the bank to cover his losses.

Ibrahim Khairat asked Shaikh As-Salhubi about Abd al-Halim Pasha Shukri.

"He went abroad at the right time," the Shaikh replied, "and with the appropriate excuse. He won't be coming back, of course."

"It's no better than it is here," said Samir Abd al-Baqi. "The foreign policy page reads like the obituaries!"

"Then the world really is threatened by total destruction," Abbas Sadiq said.

"It's threatened by destruction," said Isa as he dealt the hand, "whether it's war or peace!"

"You only philosophize when you're feeling in low spirits," Shaikh As-Salhubi said with a laugh. "Maybe your flood of good luck is drying up!"

Isa lost the round even though he had three tens. "One word from you," he told the Shaikh angrily, "would bring a whole town bad luck."

"Rubbish!" As-Salhubi replied with a laugh. "I've chased the present generation with my blessed words since the day it was born. And just look what's happened to it!"

Isa put his whole heart and soul into the game. He enjoyed the ardor, hope, enthusiasm, and absorption of it all with a languid vitality. Everything was forgotten, even history and the disasters which it had brought with it. He joined pleasure in its crazy existence. There was at least seven pounds on the table. He pinned his hopes on a solitary ace and then drew a card. There was the ace smiling at him with its red face. But then Ibrahim threw down his flush like a thunderbolt. His nervous system leapt several times, just as it had done on the day when the dissolution of the political parties was announced. He wondered what his wife was doing at that moment; would she be talking to her mother? Maybe the old

woman would be telling her that they had accepted their particular problem, but it did not seem to have accepted them.
He's out of work, she would be saying, expelled because of
his bad reputation; and he doesn't worship God either. Too
bad for Qadriyya if she got in his way. She had been married
several times and was barren, naturally barren, and she was
at least ten years older than him too!

When he came to himself again, Shaikh As-Salhubi was
carrying on with what he had been saying earlier. "That's
why we're in the age of fundamental principles," he was saying, "just like the days when the great religions were in conflict with each other!"

"What hope have the small nations got in life," asked Samir Abd al-Baqi, "if the great nations don't disagree with
each other?"

"The atom is the flood," Shaikh As-Salhubi said with conviction. "Either we turn in truth to Almighty God, or else
there will be 'clear destruction'!"*

Isa tried hard to remember where he had come across that
idea before, the idea of the flood. He forgot this philoso-
phizing when he found four tens in his hand. He sprang into
action so as to make up for his losses during the long night.
He opened with twenty-five piasters to draw them into the
round, but they all passed because they had such poor
hands. His head was spinning. Then he showed his winning
hand.

"Your luck's worse when you're winning than when
you're losing!" shouted Ibrahim Khairat.

"You're undoubtedly lucky in love," Shaikh As-Salhubi remarked.

Isa was about to boil over. Gambling can eventually become a deadly disease, he told himself. He started to reckon
up what kind of crisis was waiting for him at home. Everyone
stopped playing just as dawn was about to appear.

Abbas Sadiq stood up. "What fun would there be at Ra's al-Barr," he said, "if it weren't for gambling?"

Isa went out into the street feeling like a candle with only the vestige of the wick left. Abbas Sadiq and Samir Abd al-Baqi walked one way, and he walked another with Shaikh As-Salhubi. A dewy breeze blew quietly, and the sounds of people sleeping happily resounded in a darkness broken only by the light of the stars and by the moon rising at the end of the month. From afar, the horizon echoed the roaring of the sea. Shaikh As-Salhubi yawned as he intoned the word "Allah." "How beautiful it is at this time of night," he murmured.

"Especially when you've won!" Isa replied with a laugh.

"I've left this evening session of ours with no wins or losses," the Shaikh said with a laugh. "Abbas Sadiq is God's own lighted fire." Then, after a pause: "Isa, you're a risky gambler, you know!"

"I lost," Isa replied with a tone full of meaning, "even though I had a pair of aces in my right hand."

The Shaikh realized what he meant. "That's the way the world is," he replied. "Do we deserve the things that happen to us? Let's admit that we do make mistakes, but then, who doesn't? How can this renegade nation have forgotten us? How can it forget the people who used to treat it as a sympathetic mother treats her only child?"

A feeling of sadness overwhelmed Isa and his willful pride softened. "We were a party with the very loftiest ideals," he said, responding to a sudden desire to make a confession, "a party of self-sacrifice and absolute integrity. In the face of all kinds of temptations and threats, we were the party which said, 'No, and no again.' We were like that before 1936. So how did our pure spirit get so senile? How did we sink little by little till we had lost all the good qualities we had? Now here we are turning up our hands in despair in the darkness, feeling sad and guilt-stricken. It's too bad."

"We were the best of them all," the Shaikh said insistently, "right up till the very last moment."

"That's a relative judgment," Isa replied in a bitter tone which was really aimed at himself. "It doesn't fit in with the nature of things, nor does it satisfy the people who are tackling life so enthusiastically. Too bad, then . . ."

Isa said good night to him at the end of the street. He watched him as he walked slowly away with the wind blowing in his loose-fitting *gallabiyya*. The Shaikh had started his life, Isa thought sadly, by being imprisoned in Tanta when the Australian soldiers had arrested him as he was shouting. "Long live the homeland . . . long live Saad." He had ended up in 1942 trading in vacant jobs, just as I finished up with bank account number 33123 at the Bank of Egypt.

He looked up at the universe. The rising moon was shining brightly, and the stars were gleaming, infinity overwhelming everything else. "What does it all mean?" he asked himself in an audible voice. "Tell me; my guide's all confused."

The doorbell rang loudly in the nocturnal silence when he pressed it. He waited for a while, then rang it again. He waited, and then rang again. He kept on pressing the bell, but there was no answer. She must have decided not to open the door! he thought. He stamped on the ground, then turned around and walked away.

TWENTY-SEVEN

He spent the night at Ibrahim Khairat's house. The next day he took a room in the Grand Hotel on the Nile. After a week he had to draw another hundred pounds to cover his never-ending losses and his daily expenses. Ibrahim's wife went to see Qadriyya at her husband's suggestion to apologize for the unintentional role which Ibrahim had played in her quarrel with her husband. Then she tried to bring about a reconciliation, but got no response. Isa kept on gambling without the slightest consideration of the consequences. Samir stopped coming to their evening sessions because he was so disgusted by the dissipation he could see in his friend. "You should really take a look at your entire situation," he told Isa one day.

They were sitting in the Soprano Casino overlooking the sea. It was noon, the time of day when he usually woke up. With his round eyes, Isa was following a group of swimming girls. He did not comment on his friend's remark, but continued enjoying the view. Samir repeated what he had said.

"I'd really like to try an experiment," Isa said, "one that has never been possible at the right time. I'd like to flirt with a pretty girl and get to know her, then propose to her. Meanwhile, we'd be exchanging presents, talking to each other, and making promises to each other over the telephone."

"Do you really want to get married again?" Samir asked him.

He looked up at a slow-moving cloud which had a shape like a camel. "Just look at that cloud," he said. "Tell me, is it possible that our life was created like that shape up there?"

"Even that fleeting shape is inevitable," Samir replied with a smile. "It's the result of hundreds of different factors of air and nature. But tell me, do you want to get married?"

Isa laughed and finished his Spatis.* "Just a dream," he said. "Why do Sufis always believe everything?"

"Well, then," Samir said angrily, "let's discuss your situation."

"Just imagine," Isa replied in a similar tone, "as I was coming from the hotel, I met Sami Pasha Abd ar-Rahman, the old Free Constitutionalist. I felt rather attached to him personally because we both belonged to the past generation. We shook hands with each other and stood there talking. Strangely enough, if it hadn't been for Saad Zaghlul, we wouldn't have got into this situation!"

Samir laughed so loudly that lots of people sitting around stared at them.

"The biggest trick I let them pull on me was the dowry balance," Isa said in a different tone of voice. "The old woman's a farsighted old devil!"

"Qadriyya Hanem is a very reasonable woman, Isa," Samir said sorrowfully. "You're mad to be doing all this gambling."

Isa breathed in angrily. "It's boredom," he muttered.

"Work and work again," said Samir, patting his hand. "That's my first and last piece of advice to you."

Samir came in at the very beginning of the evening session, when Isa was concentrating on the game, and invited him to accompany him on some urgent and important business. Isa tried to ignore the invitation and continue playing, but Samir dragged him from the table in spite of his cries of protest and the silent protests of the people around him as well.

He found himself in Samir's chalet confronted by Ihsan, Samir's wife, and Qadriyya, his own wife, who was sitting on a large chair with her head lowered. Ihsan welcomed him and sat him down next to her on a long, ornate semicircular sofa. "Thank you so much for coming," she said. She gestured at Qadriyya Hanem. "May I present to you a dear friend of mine. She's married to a fine man who's been lost in action."

Isa frowned and Qadriyya blushed. Her eyes moistened, and Samir noticed it. "That's a good sign," he said. "What do you say?"

They did not stop speaking for a single moment. "Every problem can be solved without an argument," Ihsan said.

"Things can be put right again with a little kindness," Samir told Qadriyya with a smile. "Your husband is a stubborn man. In the past, he was subjected to all kinds of terror and torture without changing his mind."

"Are you happy with this situation?" Qadriyya asked. "Tell me."

A silver tray with *cassata* cakes and pastries from the local market was passed around. There was a pause while they ate.

"Humanity as a whole needs some doses of Sufism," Samir said. "Without it, life would lose its pleasure."

"We need to come back to life several times," said Isa, "till we perfect it."

Qadriyya now spoke to him for the first time. "I hope you're not holding back your kindness toward me till some other life, then," she said.

Samir had moistened the edge of his handkerchief with water and was using it to rub his trouser leg at the knee where a drop of strawberry juice had spilled. "Let's talk about the future," he suggested. "Please . . ."

"I'm quite sure," Qadriyya said, "that the only thing that could get him out of his difficulties is a job. I'll accept any sacrifice to achieve that much!"

"I completely agree with you," Samir said. "But he must

move away from Ra's al-Barr so that that excellent idea can sink in. You've spent the month of August here; that's enough. Go to Alexandria and spend the rest of the summer there. That seems both essential and urgent."

"We'll leave tomorrow," Qadriyya said, "provided he agrees."

"You'll find ample time to think in Alexandria," Samir said as he led them to the outside door of the chalet. "When you get back to Cairo in October, you'll start work immediately."

They walked side by side in the street, which was almost empty. The half-moon was fixed above the horizon like a cosmic smile in a clear sky. He had a thought; all that beauty scattered around in such remarkable order was just some unknown, mocking force, compelling mankind to realize the intensity and chaos of its own misery.

"I've found out that I've got high blood pressure," Qadriyya muttered, "and you're the cause of it all!"

"Really?"

"Yes. The doctor examined me and gave me some medicine and put me on a diet."

"I hope you'll soon get better," he told her, stroking her back very gently. He felt he was not getting any further in his quest for happiness. A marriage with no love, a life without hope. Even if he did have some success with a job, he would still be out of work.

TWENTY-EIGHT

The two of them traveled to Alexandria alone, and her mother stayed on in Ra's al-Barr. They lived in the Louvre Hotel for a few days till Isa found a flat in Sidi Gaber on the seventh floor of a building overlooking the sea. The summer season was almost over; there was less noise to be heard from young people now, and the skies were welcoming masses of white clouds. The weather was conducive to peace and contemplation. Qadriyya seemed to be really happy even though she felt unwell. She stuck to her diet in spite of her fondness for food. If it took off some of her weight, she said, then so much the better. Isa grew fond of walking and avoided eating fatty foods as much as possible so that he could regain his slim appearance. They both agreed that he would start work as soon as he returned to Cairo. He had decided to open an office, although the idea did not seem to fill him with a great deal of pleasure. "I'd really like some other kind of life," he said.

She stared inquiringly into his face with her huge, cowlike eyes.

"Don't get worried," he resumed hurriedly. "That's just a dream. I'd like to live in the country, far away from Cairo; I'd only like to see it on special occasions. I'd like to spend the day working in the fields and the night on a balcony looking out on space and silence."

"But we've no connections with the countryside," she said in alarm.

"It's just a dream."

Days went by, and he felt exasperated. All he got from the

almost deserted beaches was a lonely feeling, especially since Qadriyya preferred to stay in the house most of the time because of her health. He used to walk till his feet felt tired; when he sat down, it would be in the Gleem Paradise, where he could hang on to his memories. His own era was over, he told himself, and he wouldn't be able to merge into the same kind of life as he had had before. Here he was, tied to a woman in order to steal from her, not love her. He wondered when the world was going to be wiped out, and whether there wasn't some other kind of ideas which might give his heart some life again.

He found a palm reader in Indian dress standing in front of him, looking at him with gleaming eyes. He was sitting in his usual place in the Paradise. He stretched out his hand, and the man brought over a seat and sat down in front of him. He started concentrating immediately on the lines of his palm, while Isa waited patiently for the voice of the occult with a smile of resignation.

"You'll have a long life," the man said, "and you'll recover from a serious illness." He looked at his hand again. "You'll marry twice," he continued, "and have children."

Isa listened with interest. The man continued. "There are many upsets in your life," he said, "but you've nothing to fear because you have a will of iron. But you, you'll risk being drowned at sea!"

"At sea?"

"That's what your palm says. You're an ambitious man without any consideration for others. You'll always find an abundant means of support, but your nervousness often spoils your peace of mind."

The man stood up, bending his head in farewell as he did.

"What's the way out?" Isa asked him without thinking as he was about to leave.

The man looked at him inquisitively. Isa scoffed at himself and gave him a thankful gesture.

In the evening, he started walking along the Corniche till he reached Camp Cesare.* There was a row of cafés and shops which were bunched together on the pavement in a riot of lights, and it was there that his eyes fell on Riri! He stopped dead in his tracks on the Corniche. Fear gripped him as he looked again more carefully. Yes, it was definitely Riri, no one else. She was in a small place which sold ice cream and *ful** and *taamiyya** sandwiches, and was sitting behind the till on the chair belonging to either the manager or the owner. He rested his back on the seawall at a spot out of the light and scrutinized her face in amazement. When he recalled the way he had behaved, he felt very uncomfortable—he was shocked by how cruel and unpleasant he had been to her. Riri! It was Riri, no one else; but she was no longer a girl. Certainly not! She was a woman now in every sense of the word, and had a personality of her own—which the waiter who kept moving to and fro with orders between her and the customers obeyed to the full. A serious woman and a real manager. The incredible thing was that he had walked this way for twenty days in succession without looking at this small place. Now he read the name clearly: Take It and Thanks. On the few occasions when he had spent the summer in Alexandria, he had thought of her and been worried about the idea of meeting her either by himself or with his wife and friends. But he had found no sign of her. Eventually he had come to the conclusion that she had left town or maybe the world altogether. How had it come about that she was sitting in that seat? Were five years enough—without a world war—for her to reach this level? Her teacher in Al-Ibrahimiyya would undoubtedly be jealous of the rapid way she had advanced. Her colleagues would never have dreamed of it!

He stood there in the semi-darkness, not taking his eyes off her, and recalled their old relationship which was now forever lost in the recesses of oblivion. The superficiality of human relationships amazed him. Without realizing it, he thought, we're trying out death; we experiment with it time after time during our lives before death finally catches up with us. The whole scene with Riri sitting there in her place looked just like the Saadi Club when he used to walk in front of it, or like the House of Parliament. They were all lives destined to an early death, and the only things to benefit from them would be insects.

A woman in servant's clothes came into the place leading a little girl by the right hand. She went and spoke seriously to Riri. Meanwhile the little girl jumped onto Riri's lap and started playing lovingly and trustingly with the necklace she was wearing. At that moment, Isa had a thought that made his heart pound so much that it even covered the noise of the sea behind him. His whole body went rigid, and he looked closely at the little girl. He lost all consciousness of what was around him. But no . . . no! Why was his head spinning like this? What a stupid thought, and terrifying too! The little girl's face was turned toward her mother, so he could not see it. Things would pass quietly, he told himself, and then he would laugh at himself after it was all over. But the earth had already slipped and everything standing had been destroyed. Well, then, he should run, and never come back to Camp Cesare again, never return to Alexandria. He did not budge a single inch from the spot where he was standing. How had these idiotic ideas managed to take him by surprise?

Riri released herself from the little girl, kissed her, and then put her on the ground. The servant took hold of her hand and led her out of the café. She made for a side street that went inland from the shore. Instead of running away, he dashed across the road toward the side street and kept quickening his pace till he almost caught up with the two of them. He could hear the little girl piping up with some unintelligible words, almost all of them unintelligible except for "chocolate"; she sounded just like a chirping sparrow. They stopped in front of a shop on the corner of a cross street which sold sweets and games. He took up position next to her in the gleaming light, and asked for a box of cigarettes. He began to scrutinize the girl's face with an avid curiosity. Did not her face have a triangular shape to it? And those circular eyes! The features of his mother and three sisters were all mingled in hers; they seemed to come and go. Was it just his imagination? Was it fear? Or was it the truth? He almost collapsed from sheer exhaustion. His heart was pounding fast, sending out continuous waves of amazement, disgust, panic, grief, longing, and desire for death.

The servant took her away to a building which faced the shop on the other side of the street. He gazed after them till they disappeared. Breathing heavily, he looked up at the sky, and then muttered, "Mercy . . . mercy . . ."

TWENTY-NINE

He sat down in the Eagle Café, near Riri's place, to avoid being seen by her. He was very sorry that he had not spoken to the servant or the little girl, and had not been able for a single moment to shake himself out of the paralysis which had gripped him. The girl was sweet, energetic, and dainty; wasn't her age consistent with the whole sad episode? What could he do now? He could not postpone his answer; the past was becoming more and more loathsome, and the thought of going back to Qadriyya was too awful to even be considered. He totally abandoned the idea of running away; he had got used to running several times a day, but he would not do so in the face of this new reality which had stirred up the turgid marsh of his own life till it burst out from free springs. Maybe it was a final despairing invitation to a life with some meaning—a meaning he had failed to find anywhere. No, this time he would not run away; he could not do so. He would face reality defiantly, and at any price; yes, at any price at all. How he would welcome it! Qadriyya would certainly be able to find another man to live under her wing. She deserved affection, it was true, but the false life which he had lived with her did not merit it. It was futile to carry on with such a life, mulling over past fancies without any future. His heart never throbbed with love for anything, but now here was a golden opportunity for it to throb till he died. The little girl was his own daughter; in a few minutes he would know the truth. He would not condemn her to the same orphaned state which history had decreed for him. A veritable bomb would explode in his life because of her; remarks, rumors, and thoughts, all these things would make him the talk of the town. However, he would steel himself to the ordeal; he would suffer, make amends, and then he would live. Eventually he would find a meaning in life. If and when he could join up with his real family, he would stay in Alexandria, invest his money in this little place, and start a new life. He suppressed his shame, pride, and stubbornness, and faced life courageously.

He waited until it was past midnight. The Corniche was empty, or almost so. The people who were sitting around went away. He noticed people cleaning up in Riri's place, getting ready to close. He went over to the side street that went up into town; he stood at the corner facing the building. A figure appeared at the end of the street; it was Riri approaching. He moved forward a step till he was under the light so that she could make out his features. She came nearer, but did not pay any attention to him as he stood there. She did not bother with dawdlers anymore; that was very good.

"Riri," he said in a gentle, quavering voice as she was about to walk past him.

She stopped and looked at him. "Who are you?" she asked.

He moved a step closer. She stared at him without showing any signs of emotion. "I'm Isa," he replied.

She was looking really fit, coy and attractive. There was little doubt that she remembered him; at least, the way in which she looked so shocked, then frowned, tightened her lips, and showed her disgust indicated that she did. She was about to move on, but he blocked her path.

"Who are you?" she yelled angrily. "What do you want?"

"I'm Isa, as you know very well!"

"I don't know you," she replied, her face betraying all kinds of different emotions.

"Of course you do," he replied ardently. "There's no reason for you to deny it! I don't expect you to accept excuses, but we've some things to talk about."

"I don't know you; let me pass."

"We must talk," he said desperately. "There's no other way. I'm much more miserable than you can possibly imagine!"

"Go away," she replied angrily, "get lost! That's the best thing you can do!"

"But I'm almost going out of my mind. Who's the little girl, Riri?"

"Which little girl?"

"The one who came and sat on your lap a few hours ago, and then came into this building with her nanny. I noticed you quite by chance, and then I saw her. I followed her until she went into the building. I'm more miserable than you can imagine, I assure you."

"I don't know what you're talking about," she replied emphatically. "Go away; that's the best thing you can do!"

"I'm almost going out of my mind. You must say something. She's my daughter, Riri. You must tell me."

"Get out of my sight," she yelled in the silent street. "You're both blind and mad! Get lost, will you!"

"But my heart has told me everything."

"It's a liar, like you! That's all there is to it."

"You must tell me. I'm going crazy. I realize I've been despicable, but you've got to tell me. Tell me the girl's my daughter."

"The only thing I've got to say to you is: Get lost!"

"I know I deserve to roast in hell, but now I've a chance to do something good. Please don't make me lose it!"

"Go away," she yelled in a voice like a hurricane, "and don't let me see your face again."

"Riri, listen to me. Can't you see that I'm asking you to say something? Even if I died . . ."

"Go to hell! I warn you; get out of my way!" She rushed past him and dashed toward the door of the building.

THIRTY

He returned home before dawn after spending ages wandering along the Corniche by himself. He did not hear the sound of the waves, nor did he notice a single star. He found Qadriyya still awake waiting for him. She looked extremely anxious and annoyed. He was on the point of confessing everything to her; had he noticed any sign of encouragement from his conversation with Riri, he would have done so. But all he could tell Qadriyya was that he had been trying to resist his bad habits and had felt the need to hang around on the Corniche till dawn. "Damn it all," he told himself as he flung himself on the bed, "I must pull this false life out by the roots. Either there's got to be a new life, or else there's no escape; it'll be back to the gambling, cognac, and old women's chatter in the corner of El Bodega."

He went begrudgingly with her to the Rio cinema the next day in the evening, and then they ate dinner in a tavern. Afterwards they went home, and he made to go out. "Go to sleep, my dear," he told her, "sleep well and leave me to cure myself."

He hovered for a long time around Riri's place and in front of the building in case he might catch a glimpse of the little girl, but without success. He sat down in the Eagle Café. In spite of his failure the day before, there was still a vague hope that kept toying with him as though he were drunk. He believed that tonight all the world's problems would be solved without any trouble. He looked up at the sky, obscured by dark clouds, and told himself that autumn in Alexandria had a spirit of paradise about it to wash away all sorrows; they were merely illusions, and death was the guardian of eternal happiness. "How marvelous," he whispered to himself, "to be drunk without drinking any wine."

A bootblack was standing in front of him and giving him a pleading look. Isa noticed him and read more than one meaning in the look which the man was giving him. Isa gestured to him to sit down and then gave him his shoes to shine. He was eager to console himself by confirming his idea about this man. "Are there any vacant flats around?" he asked.

"At this time of year," the man replied with a smile, "there are more flats available than worries in a man's heart!"

"I'm really looking for a vacant room."

"In a pension?"

"I'd prefer a family!" Isa replied with a wink.

The man smiled and relaxed a little. "There are more families around too than worries in a man's heart!"

Isa laughed happily. Then he had a thought and pointed toward Riri's place. "What about the proprietress of Take It and Thanks?"

The man's expression changed. "No, no!" he replied earnestly. "She's a proper woman in every sense of the word."

Isa looked at him in a way that seemed to be telling him to continue.

"Don't waste your time," the man said. "I've nothing to do with her."

"You don't understand me," Isa replied. "One look at her is enough to confirm what you're saying. She has a lovely little girl."

"Yes, Ni'mat. She's her daughter and she's legitimate too!"

Isa smiled, trying to look unconcerned. "But you never see her father," he said. "Isn't she married?"

"Of course. Her husband owns the place."

"Why doesn't he run it himself?"

"He's in prison," the man replied after a moment's hesitation.

"What for?"

"Drugs! He's been done an injustice, I swear by God."

"May the good Lord release him! But are you sure he's the child's father?"

A cautious look flashed across the man's eyes. "Of course!" he replied.

"No, no!" Isa said with a brash confidence. "Either you know the truth and refuse to admit it," he continued with a laugh, "or else I know more than you do."

"What do you know?"

"I'd like to hear it from you. Otherwise, how can we do any business with one another if you start off by lying to me?"

The bootblack put polish on Isa's shoes. "They say," he replied with resignation, "that the good man wrote his name on the birth certificate!"

"But why?"

"He's old and a good man. He had no children and loved the woman. So he married her in the proper way!"

"A good man indeed," Isa replied, finding it hard to swallow his saliva. "He doesn't deserve to be in prison."

"That's why she keeps the place going and waits for him patiently and loyally."

"He deserves that and more," said Isa. He gave the man ten piasters and wished him well for the future.

After midnight he waited under the lamp. She spotted him as she was approaching, frowned angrily, and moved away from where he was standing.

"I've been waiting," he pleaded. "It's been agony for me. We must talk."

She walked on without answering, and so he stood in her way. "She's my daughter," he said. "At least tell me that."

"I'll yell for the police," she said angrily.

"She's my daughter! I know the whole truth."

"I'll yell for the police. Aren't you listening?"

"You should yell mercy and forgiveness instead."

She cowed him with a flood of abuse. "Hellfire's what you deserve," she retorted, "not forgiveness."

"Let's look for a way to forget the past."

"I've forgotten it entirely. Now you disappear with it!"

"Listen, Riri. You're waiting in vain. You'll get your freedom and then . . ."

"What a lousy wretch you are!" she interrupted furiously. "Just as you always were. Can't you ever imagine anything good?"

He screwed up his face in pain. "It really has been agony for me," he groaned.

"Your agonies are no business of mine," she replied bitterly.

"She's my daughter. She's got nothing to do with that man in prison."

Riri looked at him aghast but soon recovered her composure. "She's his daughter," she replied. "He adopted her because of his own ideas about what's right. She belongs to him forever and so do I."

He screwed up his face even more.

"Just make sure you don't meet me again after this," she said threateningly. "I'm warning you . . ."

"You're closing the door of mercy, Riri."

"You closed it yourself. So get lost."

"But my daughter . . ." he said tearfully.

"You're not a father," she retorted as she rushed on her way. "You're a coward; you could never be a father!"

THIRTY-ONE

He stood there hiding behind the side of a cabin on the beach at Camp Cesare, stealing furtive looks at them. Riri was sitting under an umbrella with her arms folded, and little Ni'mat was bending over the sand a few yards away, eagerly digging a pit. It was a clear morning, and the sun covered the meager gathering of people scattered over the beach; it was a gentle, kindly sun, brightened by an invigorating breeze. He kept out of her sight, so much so that no one would have realized he had come. His heart melted as he looked at the little girl and he wanted to kiss her and then disappear forever. Her body was tiny but well formed, a woman's shape in miniature. Her tanned legs, her thighs, her long hair wet at the ends, her uncovered sides, her orange bathing costume, and her total involvement in what she was doing, it was all incredible and marvelous; and she was really happy. There she was, the fruit of boredom on his part and fear on the part of her mother; and yet, from these two reprehensible qualities, life had created an attractive being, overflowing with health and happiness. The hidden power's will had decreed, and all obstacles had collapsed in the face of the eternal, enigmatic awakening. This little girl was a sure sign of the idiocy of many fears, a token of nature showing us how it is possible to overcome corruption. Now, he thought, can't you imitate nature, just once? From your sorrows, losses, and defeats, can't you make a victory, even if it's just a modest one? It's nothing rare or new. The sea has kept its appearance for millions of years and seen countless examples of it, and so has the clear blue sky.

Finally he left his hiding place and moved toward the little girl without worrying about Riri, who was standing up to face him. He sank down on the sand beside the little girl. She was alarmed by the suddenness of it all, but even so he planted a long, warm kiss on her cheek. Then he muttered, "Farewell," and left without turning back.

When lunchtime came, he did not feel like going home, and so he ate at 'Ala Kaifak. At three o'clock, he went to the cinema and then at six to another one. Afterwards he went back to 'Ala Kaifak to have dinner and drink some cognac. He sat there for a long time; the wine seeped into his head and made him feel drunk. He felt comforted by the view and by his own dreams.

Just before midnight, he saw someone coming toward the restaurant who attracted his attention like an electric shock. It was a tall, muscular, dark young man, wearing gray trousers and a white short-sleeved shirt and carrying a red rose between the fingers of his left hand. He came up close to the restaurant with a strong, graceful stride. There was a bold, piercing look in his eyes and they exchanged glances as he entered the place. He stared at Isa intently, and Isa realized that he recognized him. Then with something akin to a smile the man averted his face with its elongated features, and went to the fruit juice corner.

It was he and no one else. From the war days. One night, he had arrested this young man, and until dawn he had attended the inquest himself in his official and party capacity. The young man had been bold and stubborn, and the inquest had not found him guilty. He had been sent to prison anyway and had stayed there till the ministry had resigned. What could he be doing now? Had he secured a senior position in the new regime? Or was he still a revolutionary? Why had he smiled? It was quite clear that he remembered him; should he expect some sudden act of violence? He decided to put the man out of his mind, but some irresistible impulse made him turn toward the fruit juice corner. He saw the man standing there facing toward the inside of the place; he was holding a glass of mango juice in his right hand and looking inquisitively in his direction. His eyes seemed to smile sarcastically. Isa looked outside again; he felt utterly depressed. It was as though, with that look, the past were pursuing him.

Before long he got up and left the place. He headed straight for the Corniche. It did not occur to him to go home; indeed it seemed to him that he no longer had any home at all. After walking a considerable way, he headed toward the square and sat on a bench under Saad Zaghlul's statue. Most of the benches were empty. The cold breeze blew gently around the wide square and toyed with the palm trees. The stars were shining in the enormous vault above him, and the night was as fixed as eternity itself. He had not yet succeeded in erasing the memory of the young man from his mind, but he resolved to devise a plan for the future. However, he had hardly buried himself in his own dreams when he was aware of someone sitting by his side. He looked around with a suppressed feeling of annoyance and saw the defiant young man. He started in alarm, thinking that he must have followed him every step of the way and was planning to do him some harm. He sprang up to defend himself but at the same time felt ashamed at the thought of slinking away. Just then, the young man spoke to him in a throaty voice. "Good evening, Ustaz* Isa," he said kindly, "or rather, good morning; it's a few minutes past midnight."

Isa looked at him coldly in the gleam of a distant light. "Good morning," he replied. "Who are you?"

"You remember me, of course!"

"I'm very sorry," said Isa, feigning amazement, "who are you?"

The young man laughed as if to say, "You know, and so do I!" "Enemies are the very last people you forget!" he said.

"I don't understand what you're talking about."

"Yes, you do! You remember the inquest that went on till morning. Then I was sent to prison. Even you used to put free people in prison. Unfortunately . . ."

"I don't know precisely what you're talking about," Isa replied, retreating a little, "but I certainly remember the war days and the harsh circumstances which often forced us to do things we didn't like doing."

"That's the traditional excuse. Never mind! What's past is past."

Isa did not say a word, but looked straight ahead to make it clear that he wished to be left alone, in the hope that the other man would go away and leave him in peace. But he started talking again. "The world has changed," the man said gently. "Don't think I'm being malicious. I would never do a thing like that, I promise you. But I often feel sorry . . ."

"I don't need your sympathy," Isa interrupted somewhat angrily.

"Don't get angry and misunderstand my reasons for intruding on you. I would like to discuss things seriously with you."

"What?"

"The world around us!"

Isa realized that he was still drunk. "Nothing bothers me anymore," he said.

"It's quite the opposite with me," the young man replied. "Everything concerns me; I think about everything . . ."

"Then I hope the world turns out as you wish."

"Isn't that better than sitting in the dark under Saad Zaghlul's statue?"

"That's fine as far as I'm concerned. Don't bother about me."

"You haven't made up your mind to open your heart to me yet."

"Why should I? Don't you see that the whole world's a bore?"

"I haven't got time to be bored."

"What are you doing then?"

"I make a joke of the troubles I used to have, and look ahead with a smile. I smile in spite of everything; so much that you might think I was mad."

"What makes you smile?"

"Incredible dreams," the young man replied in a still more earnest tone. "Let's choose somewhere better to talk."

"I'm sorry," Isa replied quickly. "Actually I've already had two glasses of cognac and now I need some rest."

"You want to sit in the dark under Saad Zaghlul's statue," the young man replied regretfully.

Isa did not say a word. The young man stood up to leave. "You don't want to talk to me," he said. "I shouldn't pester you anymore." He walked away in the direction of the city.

Isa watched him as he left. What an odd young man! I wonder what he's doing now, he thought. Had those troubles really taken pity on him? Why was he looking ahead with a smile? He kept watching the young man till he reached the edge of the square. He had not meant him any harm after all. Why didn't I encourage him to talk? Maybe I should ask him to help me overcome my boredom, even at this hour of the night. Our conversation might lead us into an adventure that would brighten up the night.

He saw the young man disappear in the direction of Safiyya Zaghlul Street. I could catch up with him, he thought, if I didn't waste any more time hesitating. He jumped to his feet in a sudden drunken spurt of enthusiasm and started after the young man with long strides, leaving the seat behind him sunk in solitude and darkness.

NOTES

'Ala Kaifak: the name means "as you like" or "whatever you like," and may have some symbolic significance—perhaps suggesting Isa's nihilism.

Athenios: a café-restaurant in Alexandria.

Al-Azarita: a district of Alexandria, also known as Al-Mazarita.

bawwab: doorman.

Bey: title of respect for important men, from the Turkish; formerly the title of the governor of a small Ottoman province. Went out of official use in Egypt after the 1952 revolution, but continues as a polite mode of address and reference.

Camp Cesare: a district of Alexandria.

casino: not a place to gamble, but a teahouse or restaurant, especially one along the Corniche in Alexandria or along the river in Cairo. A local evolution from the European-style casinos established around Azbakiya in the nineteenth century.

"clear destruction": the Arabic adjective *mubiin* (clear, obvious, self-evident) is used many times in the Qur'an, thus giving this phrase a "Qur'anic" flavor.

colocynth: a bitter fruit.

condemned man in the mountain: in Egyptian Arabic, the word for "mountain" is often used to mean "desert," "wasteland," or, to Nile Valley residents, far-off, isolated areas such as the desert oases. Egyptian regimes have at times sent some criminals to work in areas such as these; thus "the condemned man in the mountain" would be a man sentenced to labor in the far reaches of the country.

conquian: a card game similar to rummy.

Corniche: from the French, a road passing alongside water (i.e., in Cairo, along the Nile; in Alexandria, along the Mediterranean coast).

Dokki: an upper-middle-class district of Giza, across the river from Cairo; it was then, as it is now, associated with the *nouveau arrivé*.

faqih: a reader or reciter of the Qur'an.

ful: fava beans; one of the staples of the Egyptian diet.

gallabiyya: the ankle-length garment worn by men of the lower classes in Egypt.

Gleem: a district of Alexandria.

Groppi's: a famous café-restaurant in Cairo; its proprietors were European.

Al-Hajj(a):   someone who has made the pilgrimage to Mecca (the "a" indicates a woman).

Hanem: a term of respect addressed to a woman, much as the terms Bey and Pasha are applied to a man.

Hijaz: The area of the Arabian peninsula, formerly a king-dom and now a viceroyalty, that includes Mecca and Medina. The sandalwood rosary is typical of the sort of souvenir brought back by pilgrims from the Holy Places.

Al-Ibrahimiyya: a district of Alexandria.

khamsin: the hot winds which blow off the desert in Egypt, carrying dense clouds of sand.

khwaaga: the colloquial Egyptian term for "foreigner."

Maghrebi: from the Maghreb, or northwestern Africa.

nargila: the hookah or hubble-bubble.

notable (*a'yan*): a technical term used in Ottoman and later times to denote the local families of influence.

Pasha: title of high civil or military rank used in the Ottoman Empire and continuing in official use in Egypt until the 1952 revolution. Still in use as a polite or respectful term of address.

Ra's al-Barr: a small town in the Nile Delta.

Ramla Square: the square in central Alexandria from which the trains for Ramla leave and where the Trianon restaurant is located.

Ar-Risalat al-Qushairiyya: a treatise by the famous mystic Al-Qushairi (d. 1072).

Saad: see Zaghlul.

Sakakini: a district of Cairo.

second grade: the second highest rank in the civil service; the next step would be an under-secretaryship.

Sharia: the Arabic word for "street".

Sidi Bishr: a resort district in Alexandria.

Sidi Umar: the second Caliph, renowned for his asceticism and astuteness.

Spatis: a popular Egyptian cordial.

Sufism: Islamic mysticism.

taamiyya: a pâté made from crushed beans, onions, garlic, and parsley.

Tanta: a town on the railway line midway between Cairo and Alexandria; a center of pilgrimage in Egypt.

twenty-third of July: 1952. The day on which the Army officers took over the government, disbanding Parliament and outlawing the parties.

ulama: religious scholars, particularly those who have studied at Al-Azhar, a mosque and university in Cairo which was long the center of the Islamic intellectual world.

umda: the head of the village community in Egypt, responsible for such things as tax collection and drafting villagers into the Army.

Urabi Pasha: the hero and martyr of nineteenth-century Egyptian nationalism of the 1880s, when the autonomy of the country was threatened by European concerns over investments. The nationalist movement was crushed, but never forgotten, in 1882, when British troops defeated the Egyptian Army. This uprising was also characterized by fires, as Alexandria was set ablaze by the fighting.

Ustaz: literally "professor," but used in Egyptian colloquial dialect to mean little more than "Mr."

Wafd: "delegation"; the name of the political party founded in 1919 by Saad Zaghlul which was the major political force in Egypt before the 1952 revolution.

Al-Wayiliyya: a district of Cairo.

Zaghlul, Saad: the famous Egyptian nationalist leader and Prime Minister, 1924–27; founder of the Wafd Party, to which Isa belonged.

Zizinia: a district of Alexandria.